T0326510

Digital Directions

Digital Directions

Artificial Intelligence Pathways for Higher Education

Edited by

Darrel W. Staat

ROWMAN & LITTLEFIELD
Lanham • Boulder • New York • London

Published by Rowman & Littlefield
An imprint of The Rowman & Littlefield Publishing Group, Inc.
4501 Forbes Boulevard, Suite 200, Lanham, Maryland 20706
www.rowman.com

86-90 Paul Street, London EC2A 4NE, United Kingdom

British Library Cataloguing in Publication Information Available

Library of Congress Cataloging-in-Publication Data Available

ISBN 9781475871920 (cloth : alk. paper) | ISBN 9781475871937 (paper : alk. paper) |
    ISBN 9781475871944 (ebook)

Contents

Preface

As the twenty-first century advances, a number technologies are developing right along with it, such as autonomous cars the Internet of Things, personal robots, genome development, quantum computing, nanotechnology and artificial intelligence (AI). Although all of these technologies and more to come, will influence society, culture, and daily life; however, none will have more impact than AI. The business community globally understands this, the military internationally is preparing for it, and everyone on the planet we call Earth will be affected by it in numerous ways.

Because of this wide spectrum of impacts, it is critical that those in education and, in particular, higher education become aware of AI, its potential impact, and begin now to understand how to deal with it. My research, numerous books, and presentations to educational conference attendees have made attempts to alert those in community colleges and universities of what is to come in the next decades that will literally force change in higher education as it is currently known. To ignore this technology is comparative to the ostrich with its head in the sand. To disregard AI will leave higher education in the dust.

This book attempts to convince those in higher education that disruption, phenomenal change, is heading directly for those of involved in higher education from the community college to the research university and every educational institution in between. This book creates views into the impact of AI on the present, and the futures of 2032 and of 2050. The chapters shed light on how and when AI will become part and parcel of higher education in the twenty-first century. If it is thought that change significantly modified the twentieth century, that is nothing compared to disruptions coming in the twenty-first.

Acknowledgments

I would like to express my sincere appreciate to the graduate students in cohort nine of the Higher Education Executive Leadership program at Wingate University. They spent considerable time and energy researching and writing the chapters in this book. Their devotion to study the impact of artificial intelligence on a variety of current programs in higher education has brought to the foreground some competent and innovative insights that are shared in the chapters of this book.

I would also like to thank Dr. Jeffery Frederick, Provost of Wingate University, whose keen understanding of how to lead an academic institution has led to improvements in the general operation of the institution and sincere support for the shared governance of the university. He is an inspiration to us all.

Finally, I would like to thank my dear wife, Beverly, who understands what it takes to develop the research, writing, and editing, of this book and supports my time and energy involved without question.

Introduction

The focus of this book is to glimpse into the affect that artificial intelligence (AI) will have on various programs in higher education. It starts with a brief history of AI and then moves into specific programs including education, technical programs, student affairs, agriculture, healthcare, and religion. The chapters cover the current status, an extrapolation of 2032 possibilities, and thought-provoking views into where they may be in 2050. Although not all chapters will be of interest to all readers, specific programs increase curiosity and be well worth the time to investigate. Each reader can decide to review which chapters may pique their inquisitiveness.

AI exists at present as narrow AI, that is, it has been developed for a specific purpose such as winning a chess game, winning at *Jeopardy*, suggesting books one might be interested in reading after a purchase has been made at Amazon, or determining a diagnosis and suggesting a procedure to be used for a specific medical ailment. AI is in its infancy in 2022, but it will grow and develop over the years, spurred on by quantum computing to develop in the near future through deep learning to come closer to the mind of a human being. Being aware of the development of AI keeps one from being taken advantaged by it.

The book is organized with research findings on the current status of the various topics, followed by research as to what the status most likely will be in ten years, 2032. Finally, each chapter ends with a section on where AI has the potential to exist by 2050. This section of each chapter is the result of research and estimations of where AI in the topic area may be in the foreseeable future.

The book can be read in any order, depending on the interest of the reader. Chapter 1 is an historical overview leading up to the present. The other chapters begin in the present and look forward into the future, attempting to determine where the topic may be in 2032 and 2050.

Chapter 1

Artificial Intelligence Background

Paul Mills

One of the fields destined to be affected by artificial intelligence (AI) is education. Darrel Staat (2019), author of *Exponential Technologies: Higher Education in an Era of Serial Disruptions,* reminds readers that "the world is beginning to slide toward an era of serial disruptions. What was normal in the past will evaporate like mist in the morning sun as technologies invade transportation, manufacturing, genome modification, and the definition of intelligence, to name a few" (p. vii).

Over the last few decades, faculty, students, and staff have become accustomed to encounters with AI on college campuses, whether they realize it, or not. Examples include installing bots to answering frequently asked questions on websites, automated machinery in industrial laboratories, and robots welcoming students onto college campuses has occurred at two- and four-year educational institutions of higher learning around the globe. Students in the future will use AI with more recognition of its existence and importance, and they will need to learn to work with it in their careers after graduation, as well.

Faculty and staff will need to continually stay on top of the advancement of AI and how to use it on campus in order to serve students properly. Though science fiction films have been warning of an oncoming arrival of machines and robots, which would be taking over humanity for years, it appears as if it is actually beginning to happen. Darrell West discusses how technological advances and developments in "robots, AI [artificial intelligence], virtual reality, autonomous vehicles, facial recognition algorithms, drones, and mobile sensors are altering numerous sectors and leading us to an autonomous society" (West, 2018, p. x).

Autonomous society sounds scary to some people, as it implies that humans will be unnecessary for almost any work and require major changes to the way that humans live. In *The Age of AI and Our Human Future,*

1

Kissinger et al., (2021) says that "AI's promise of epoch-making transformations—in society, economics, politics, and foreign policy—portends effects beyond the scope of any single author's or field's traditional focuses" (p. 7). These coming transformations will be so grand, that no expert will be able to comprehend how accommodating they will be.

THE JOURNEY OF AI

In order to understand the journey that the field of AI has taken, it is important to ask where and how AI became what it is today. Who is responsible for creating that first surge of information on the reality of AI? What situations were created to allow AI to grow from a concept the 1950s into the expected outcomes in the field of education in the twenty-first century? In the 1800s during the Industrial Revolution, calculation of numbers was very wearisome and often resulted in many errors due to human error and fatigue.

Charles Babbage

When Charles Babbage, a graduate of Cambridge University, initially got the idea that calculation could be mechanized and set out to prove it in 1821, he visualized a means to mechanize calculation of mathematical tables. Years after his death none of his equipment was being used regularly, and it took until the twentieth century for his ideas to become a reality. Although he did not see his vision through to reality, he did not give up. "Babbage was not an impractical technologist reaching beyond his grasp, but a creative scientist exploring ways to realize mathematical relations in mechanical form" (Collier & MacLachlan, 1999, p. 104).

Many of the units and workings of Babbage's engines were very resourceful answers to challenging complications. "As it has turned out the final complete fulfillment of the Babbage dreams depended on electrical and electronic mechanisms unavailable to him at the time . . ." (Collier & MacLachlan 1999, p. 104). Babbage never saw his ideas come to full fruition. Many years after his death, ". . . a complete machine of similar complexity to Babbage's was made in 1937, when a physicist at Harvard University, Howard Aiken, conceived of a programmable electromechanical calculating machine" (Collier & MacLachlan, 1999, p. 107).

Howard Aiken

Aiken managed to interest the United States Navy in supporting his machine and IBM designed and built it. Often referred to as the Mark I computer, when finished in 1944, it was over 50 feet long. Although it was not programmable, it was used for calculating and printing mathematical tables during World War II (Collier & MacLachlan, 1999). In 1955, Logic Theorist, considered by many to be the first AI program, was created (Ventre, 2020).

This was the outcome of collaboration between "a computer scientist (John Shaw) and two researchers from the humanities and social sciences (Herbert Simon and Allen Newell). This project, received funding from the US Air Force" (Ventre, 2020, p. 1). Ventre explains that this project had all of "the essential elements of AI research: a multidisciplinary approach, bringing together humanities and technology, a university investment and the presence of the military." He also points out "researchers never use the expression 'artificial intelligence' or present the software as falling into this category" (Ventre, 2020, p. 1).

Alan Turing

Among the other larger problems faced during World War II, a great concern involved the Nazi war machine and its ability to send decoded messages throughout Europe undecipherable by the allies. As a result of hard work by some very intelligent computer scientists, the Colossus machine was conceptualized, "designed and built in England to decode messages processed by German cipher machines" (Collier & MacLachlan, 1999, p. 108). A central individual in its scheme was Alan Turing, a forerunner in the advancement of computer theory, and a seminal figure in the AI community (Collier & MacLachlan, 1999).

Turing, best known for his work on the Theory of Computation (1937), the Turing Machine (1937), and the Turing Test (1950), is most often "credited with being the father of computer science and the father of artificial intelligence" (Cooper & Van, 2013, p. 481). Not as famously, but just as importantly, Turing is highly revered for his work in computer engineering. According to Cooper and Van (2013), Turing was more of "a mechanist concerned with getting the greatest computational power from minimal hardware resources" (p. 481).

Turing had faith in the abilities of computers; however, "he was perhaps the first to raise the question whether there are incomputable physical processes" that artificial thinking must require (Cooper & Van, 2013, p. 656). According to Kissinger, et al. (2021), "in 1943, when researchers created the first modern computer—electronic, digital, and programmable—their achievement gave new urgency to intriguing questions: Can machines think? Are they intelligent? Could they become intelligent?" (p. 48). Turing picked up on these questions.

"In 1950," says Kissinger et al., (2021), "Alan Turing offered a solution. In a paper unassumingly titled computing machinery and intelligence, Turing suggested setting aside the problem of machine intelligence entirely" (p. 48). Turing suggested that it was not the mechanism that was the problem, it was the manifestation. Turing said that "because the inner lives of other beings remain unknowable, [. . .] our sole means of measuring intelligence should be external behavior" (Kissinger, et al., 2021, p. 48).

Turing came up with a test to assess a machine's ability to think. "The 'imitation game' he introduced proposed that if a machine operated so proficiently that observers could not distinguish its behavior from a human's, the machine should be labeled intelligent [and] the Turing test was born" (Kissinger, et al., 2021, p. 48). The Turing "test has proven useful in assessing intelligent machines performance." Rather than requiring total indistinguishability from humans, it is explained that "the test applies to machines whose performance is *humanlike* . . . it focuses on performance, not process" (Kissinger, et al., 2021, p. 49).

John McCarthy

In 1956, John McCarthy, a computer scientist, ". . . defined artificial intelligence as machines that can perform tasks that are characteristic of human intelligence" building on his ideas and those around him. "Turing's and McCarthy's assessments of artificial intelligence have become benchmarks [since the 1950s], shifting our focus and defining intelligence to performance, [or] intelligent-seeming behavior" rather than a process that can be considered humanlike (Kissinger, et al., 2021, p. 49).

After playing a substantial part in delineating the field dedicated to the fostering of intelligent pieces of machinery capable of helping humans, John McCarthy, an American computer scientist forerunner and designer, was called the Father of Artificial Intelligence. In McCarthy's presentation at the 1956 Dartmouth Conference, the first time an AI conference was being held, the scientist created the expression, AI (Chakraborty, 2021). "The intention was to see if there was a way to create a machine that could think abstractly, solve problems, and develop itself like a human," (Chakraborty, 2021, par 5).

It was McCarthy's belief that "every aspect of learning or any other feature of intelligence can, in principle, be described so precisely that a machine can be made to simulate it. Programming languages, the Internet, the web, and robots are just a few of the world's technological innovations that [McCarthy] paved the way for." He also invented "the first programming language for symbolic computation, LISP (which is still used as a preferred language in the field of AI), and [is responsible for] human-level AI and commonsense reasoning" in the field (Chakraborty, 2021, par. 6).

Conference at Dartmouth College

In 1956, a group decided to put together a meeting of computer scientists. "The aim of this scientific event was to bring together a dozen or so researchers with the ambition of giving machines the ability to perform intelligent tasks and to program them to imitate human thought" (Ventre, 2020, p. 2). The organizers of the conference at Dartmouth College in 1956 were an experienced group of people.

John McCarthy, from Dartmouth, was "involved in the Hixon Symposium on Cerebral Mechanisms in Behavior in 1948." Marvin Minsky, from Harvard, "designed SNARC, the first neural network simulator" and Claude Shannon, of Bell Labs, was a "mathematics and electronics specialist" (Ventre, 2020, p. 2). McCarthy, "had attended the 1948 Symposium on Cerebral Mechanisms in Behavior," [which was also] attended by Claude Shannon, among others. This multidisciplinary symposium (mathematicians, psychologists, etc.) introduced discussions on the comparison between the brain and the computer" (Ventre, 2020, p. 3).

From a historical perspective, "the proposal for the conference . . . defines the content of the project and the very concept of artificial intelligence" (Ventre, 2020, p. 3). It reads:

> The study is to proceed on the basis of the conjecture that every aspect of learning or any other feature of intelligence can in principle be so precisely described that a machine can be made to simulate it. An attempt will be made to find how to make machines use language, form abstractions and concepts, solve kinds of problems now reserved for humans, and improve themselves. (Ventre, 2020, p. 3)

The project was considered successful even though many who were invited did not attend. The audience was composed almost entirely of North Americans—from the United States and Canada—and two from Great Britain (Ventre, 2020).

Stanford University's AI Lab

While the field of AI has changed in many essential ways since its establishment, Stanford University's AI Lab (SAIL) has become a prominent scholarly center for "scientists and engineers, an education Mecca for students, and a center of excellence for cutting edge research work" (Stanford Artificial Intelligence Lab, 2022, par. 2). SAIL, founded in 1962 by John McCarthy, is a "rich, intellectual and stimulating academic environment," that has continued to be a supportive environment for the continued research centered on AI development (Stanford Artificial Intelligence Lab, 2022, par. 1).

According to SAIL (2022), "through multidisciplinary and multi-faculty collaborations, [the institution] promotes new discoveries and explores new ways to enhance human-robot interactions through AI; all while developing the next generation of researchers" (par. 1). The staff delivers assistance to the academic and research groups at SAIL, "functioning as the strength of the lab by assisting their researchers, visiting scholars and students to advance new discoveries and innovation. These groups, working together, add to the depth and breadth of their research" (Stanford Artificial Intelligence Lab, 2022, par. 1).

Ventre (2020) says that from almost the beginning, "the Stanford AI lab has had a defense perspective in its research. US Department of Defense (DoD), subsidized the work through numerous programs" (p. 4). Military related objectives drove the research at SAIL, "as in the case of Monte D. Callero's thesis on 'An adaptive command and control system utilizing heuristic learning processes' (1967), which aimed to develop an automated decision tool for the real-time allocation of defense missiles during armed conflicts" (Ventre, 2020, p. 4).

The MIT AI Lab

The Computer Science and Artificial Intelligence Laboratory (CSAIL) at the Massachusetts Institute of Technology (MIT) "pursues fundamental research across the entire breadth of computer science and artificial intelligence" and "is committed to leading the field both in new theoretical approaches and in the creation of applications that have broad societal impact" (Massachusetts Institute of Technology, 2022, par. 1). CSAIL's current research activities covers three key topics: AI, systems, and theory are the major fields involved at CSAIL.

According to MIT (2022), the first area of research, AI, "aims to understand and develop systems—living and artificial—capable of intelligent reasoning, perception, and behavior." The specific research in this area involves "core AI computational biology, computer graphics, computer vision, human language technology, machine learning, medical informatics, robotics, and the semantic web" (Massachusetts Institute of Technology, 2022, par. 2).

The second section of research, systems, "aims to discover common principles, models, metrics, and tools of computer systems, both hardware and software" and the "specific research [in this area] includes compilers, computer architecture and chip design, operating systems, programming languages, and computer networks." The final area of specialization at CSAIL is theory. According to the institution, "This area of research studies the mathematics of computation and its consequences" (Massachusetts Institute of Technology, 2022, par. 2).

The specific research here would incorporate "algorithms, complexity theory, computations geometry, cryptography, distrusted computing, information security, and quantum computing" (Massachusetts Institute of Technology, 2022, par. 2). According to Ventre (2020), "Research at MIT in the 1970s, although funded by the military, also remained broad in its scope" (p. 5). Offering the completed research to the DoD in the early 1970s, "the researchers felt that they had reached a milestone that allowed them to envisage real applications of the theoretical work carried out until then" (Ventre, 2020, p. 5).

Geoffrey Hinton

Geoffrey Hinton, born in 1947, is a "British-Canadian cognitive psychologist and computer scientist, most noted for his work on artificial neural networks" who has, since 2013, "divided his time working for Google (Google Brain) and the University of Toronto." In 2017, according to his biography, "he co-founded and became the Chief Scientific Advisor of the Vector Institute in Toronto" (Pantheon, n.d., par. 1). Hinton is "distinguished for his work on artificial neural nets, especially how they can be designed to learn without the aid of a human teacher" (The Royal Society, n.d., par. 1).

He is well-known for his work comparing the "effects of brain damage with effects of losses in such a net, and found striking similarities with human impairment, such as for recognition of names and losses of [categorization]." His area of expertise also "includes studies of mental imagery and inventing puzzles for testing originality and creative intelligence" (The Royal Society, n.d., par. 1). Hinton is also "known by many people to be the godfather of deep learning" and "[he] has invented several foundational deep learning techniques throughout his decades-long career" (DeepLearningAI, n.d., par. 1).

DEEP LEARNING

Deep Learning basically comprises structuring or creating neural networks, which are systems that impersonates the performance of the human brain. "These multi-layered computer networks can gather information and react to it. They can build up an understanding of what objects look or sound like." "With Deep Learning," according to Daniela Hernandez (2013), inputters "give the system a lot of data so it can discover by itself what some of the concepts in the world are" (pars. 12 & 13).

In an attempt to supplement a person's vision impairment, for example, scientists might create "a basic layer of artificial neurons that can detect simple things like the edges of a particular shape," while "the next layer could then piece together these edges to identify the larger shape," and finally, "the shapes could be strung together to understand an object." Hernandez (2013) explains that "the software does all this on its own—a big advantage over older AI models, which required engineers to massage the visual or auditory data so that it could be digested by the machine-learning algorithm" (Hernandez, 2013, par. 14).

With deep learning, apparently inputs "just give the system a lot of input so it can discover by itself what some of the concepts in the world are." This method is stimulated by how it is believed that human beings learn, according to Hernandez. As infants, "we watch our environments and start to understand the structure of objects we encounter, but until a parent tells us what it is, we [cannot] put a name to it" (Hernandez, 2013, pars. 13 & 16).

HUMANS' DEPENDENCE ON ARTIFICIAL INTELLIGENCE

AI is an ally, humans are told. AI is here to help human beings to do the things that they do not want to do, or that they do not feel safe or comfortable doing. AI is here to make humans' jobs easier and to enable them to live longer and healthier lives. As most know, everyday actions for humans are dependent on AI. Kissinger et al. (2021) asserts that "social media, web searches, streaming video, navigation, ride sharing, and countless other online services could not operate as they do without the extensive and growing use of AI" (p. 79).

What complicates this is that humans "rely on AI to assist [them] in pursuing daily tasks without necessarily understanding how or why it is working at any given moment" (Kissinger et al., 2021, p. 79–80). The importance of AI grows as humans' dependence on service they cannot deliver, or even understand, exponentially increases. In an instant, almost overnight, and even "without significant fanfare—or even visibility—[people] are integrating nonhuman intelligence into the basic fabric of human activity" (Kissinger, et al., 2021, p. 80).

CONCLUSION

While Charles Babbage lit the torch, Alan Turing, John McCarthy, and Geoffrey Hinton provided the path for others to follow in pursuit of a realistic setting that would allow and support AI to become what it is today. The Dartmouth Conference of 1956 brought a few of these individuals together to collaborate and share ideas that led to the formation of two outstanding laboratories dedicated to the research and development of AI: SAIL was founded in 1962 and CSAIL was created at MIT. More recently, Geoffrey Hinton and others working with him, developed artificial neural networks , and, more specifically, used deep learning to allow full integration of AI into the lives of people around the globe.

CHAPTER SUMMARIES

- Over the last few decades, faculty, students, and staff have become accustomed to encounters with AI on college campuses, whether they realize it, or not.
- Autonomous society sounds scary to some people, as it implies that humans will be unnecessary for almost any work and require major changes to the way that humans live.
- Many of the units and workings of Babbage's engines were very resourceful answers to challenging complications.
- A central individual in its scheme was Alan Turing, a forerunner in the advancement of computer theory, and a seminal figure in the AI community.
- John McCarthy, an American computer scientist forerunner and designer, was called the Father of Artificial Intelligence.
- Geoffrey Hinton, born in 1947, is a "British-Canadian cognitive psychologist and computer scientist, most noted for his work on artificial neural networks."
- Deep learning basically comprises structuring or creating neural networks, which are systems that impersonates the performance of the human brain.
- The importance of AI grows as humans' dependence on service they cannot deliver, or even understand, exponentially increases.
- In an instant, almost overnight, and even "without significant fanfare—or even visibility—[people] are integrating nonhuman intelligence into the basic fabric of human activity."
- While Charles Babbage lit the torch, Alan Turing, John McCarthy, and Geoffrey Hinton provided the path for others to follow in pursuit of a realistic setting that would allow and support AI to become what it is today.

Paul Mills

REFERENCES

Chakraborty, M. (2021, March 1). *Knowing John McCarthy: The father of artificial intelligence*. Analytics Insight. https://www.analyticsinsight.net/knowing-john-mccarthy-the-father-of-artificial-intelligence

Collier, B., & MacLachlan, J. (1999). *Charles Babbage: And the engines of perfection*. New York, NY: Oxford University Press, Incorporated.

Cooper, S. B., & Van, L. J. (Eds.). (2013). *Alan Turing: His work and impact*. New York: NY: Elsevier Science & Technology.

DeepLearningAI. (n.d). *Heroes of deep learning: Geoffrey Hinton*. https://www.deeplearning.ai/hodl-geoffrey-hinton/#:~:text=Geoffrey%20Hinton%20is%20known%20by,of%20Toronto%20and%20Google%20Brain.

Hernandez, Daniela. (2013, May 7). *The man behind the Google brain: Andrew Ng and the quest for the new AI*. Wired. https://www.wired.com/2013/05/neuro-artificial-intelligence/

Kissinger, Henry; Schmidt, Eric; and Huttenlocher, Daniel. (2021). *The age of AI and our human future*. New York, NY Little, Brown, and Company.

Massachusetts Institute of Technology. (2022). *Computer science and artificial intelligence laboratory*. http://catalog.mit.edu/mit/research/computer-science-artificial-intelligence-laboratory/

Pantheon. (n.d.). *Computer scientist Geoffrey Hinton*. https://pantheon.world/profile/person/Geoffrey_Hinton/

The Royal Society. (n.d.). *Geoffrey Hinton*. https://royalsociety.org/people/geoffrey-hinton-11624/

Staat, Darrel. (2019). *Exponential technologies: Higher education in an era of serial disruptions*. Lanham, MD: Rowman and Littlefield.

Stanford Artificial Intelligence Lab. (2022). *About us*. https://https://ai.stanford.edu/about/

Ventre, D. (2020). *Artificial intelligence, cybersecurity and cyber defense*. New York, NY: John Wiley & Sons, Incorporated.

West, Darrell M. (2018). *The future of work: Robots, AI and automation*. Washington, D.C.: The Brookings Institution.

Chapter 2

Artificial Intelligence and Education

Kateryna Decker

The expression artificial intelligence (AI) is being used more often. Many people do not realize that AI is already present in many operations of our everyday life and is taking on more tasks that used to require humans. Those who are in schools today will face the job market of the future that will be changing constantly. Students who understand the concepts of AI and how it replicates human intelligence will be able to excel in the jobs of the future as they will be able to maximize its capabilities and transcend its limits (Zimmerman, 2018).

ARTIFICIAL INTELLIGENCE IN EDUCATION TODAY

AI is already present in schools in non-teaching as well as teaching aspects of education (Reiss, 2021). It is common to use computerized assessments that adjust the types of questions that students will work on based on the previously answered questions. Automated systems are used to calculate students' grades and provide access for students and parents to the students' records. Some schools in England use AI tools to predict addictive behaviors, self-harm, and eating disorders.

The AI-powered software administers a test twice a year using a series of abstract questions to help students ease the pressure they feel from social media. The schools that use the tool report that the incidents related to self-harm decreased by 20%. The tool helps identify students who need support. After the data from the surveys is analyzed, the students get flagged as green, yellow, or red on the teacher dashboard with the suggestion of what intervention may be needed. The general test results link students to risks of self-hurt, bullying, or not coping with pressure in about 82% of cases (Manthorpe, 2019).

Personalized Learning

There has been a great deal of anxiety lately that AI will replace human workers. Some AI development is focused on replicating human intelligence. However, most of the efforts are focused on doing what humans cannot do or finding ways to do things differently. In education, the move is to personalized learning with focus on the individual student, which differs from traditional learning approaches when everybody does one thing at the same time. Personalized learning allows creating learning programs that reflect students' interests, unique situations, cultures, and challenges (Zimmerman, 2018).

AI allows enabling greater levels of learning personalization. It expands the teacher's capacity to adjust the learning process to fit the needs of each learner. Personalized learning does not replace educators. AI-enabled technology provides data for teachers about how to guide, adjust, and let students regulate their learning process, and practice autonomy. A personalized approach to learning allows students to become innovative designers. Some AI-enabled programs like Khan Academy, Mia Learning, and Pixar in a Box are being used in schools to help teachers personalize learning (Zimmerman, 2018).

The Publishing Industry

Some book publishers started building online programs that use AI elements in their courses. McGraw Hill Mathematics has a program called ALEKS, which is used in some schools to teach math. At the beginning of the year, all students take the placement test that determines what level of math the students need to do. During the year the students work through modules at their own pace. This allows students to take more time if they need to, or to move faster. Along with practice problems, students also have recorded mini-lectures that they can listen to if they need additional expiations (Falmagne, et al., n.d.).

This approach frees teachers from delivering daily math lectures that students may be bored with. ALEKS also provides students with tips and ideas for good study habits and time management. ALEKS allows students to see how many units they have left and is based on the natural human desire to have things completed (*Research behind Aleks*. McGraw Hill ALEKS).

Chatbots

Chatbots help instructors answer repetitive questions. This allows instructors to use office hours for more complex questions. AI frees the instructor's time to work on the nuances that take place beyond the basic assessments. Professor of computer science Ashok Goel from Georgia Institute of Technology created an AI teaching assistant Jill for his online course on AI (Goel, 2017). He created a tool using an IBM platform in which about 40,000 questions were loaded from four semesters worth of data. The chatbot, TA Jill Watson, worked very well, cut the number of questions from students, and provided useful information.

Chatbots become an invaluable study resource for students. Michelle Zimmerman (2018) in her book, *Teaching AI: Exploring New Frontiers for Learning*, shares a case of a professor of mechanical engineering from the University of New South Wales in Australia who is teaching a class of 500 students; 350 students attend class in person and the rest join remotely. Professor Kellermann, his teaching assistant, and a group of tutors had to work very hard to answer the questions via chat discussions. The number of questions increased very much before final exams. There was confusion about which questions were answered, and who had to answer whom.

Professor Kellermann decided to use a bot named Question, which is now linked in the chat forum with students. Each topic from the syllabus has its channel. When students ask questions, the bot sends the request to the tutors responsible for the section. When the questions are answered, the bot cancels the request so other tutors work with unanswered questions. The bot also archives the answers and builds the knowledge base for students in the future to use, which combines the knowledge of the professor, a teaching assistant, and 12 tutors. The professor has used another AI tool that created closed captioning for all lecture recordings.

When the student asks a question the bot searches for a similar place in the video lectures and starts playing the video lecture from the moment that answers the question. This feature also helps the instructor ensure that all topics students have to review for the exams are addressed in the video lectures. When the exams come, the instructor will be able to scan each student's answers, and AI-enabled software can read and grade them. The more complicated questions are graded by tutors using rubrics. AI-enabled bots become an important resource for students. It frees instructors, and tutors' time to work on deeper questions (Zimmerman, 2018).

AI at Wingate University

Wingate University is using a Remark cloud grading tool that is built with AI elements. Instructors can prepare grading sheets for their tests based on the need of the topic they are planning to assess. After students take exams, instructors feed the answers through the scanner and upload them to the Remark cloud. Special Optical Mark Recognition technology can read barcodes, and typewriter text supports handwriting through Microsoft Computer Vision and handles cross-outs, multiple marks, and damaged forms.

The software can scan the open-ended questions if instructors provided answer options, it can read final numerical answers, and give marks for perfect calculations. If the final answer is wrong, it can flag it for a tutor review; it can mark graphs and diagrams that are correct. Instructors still review the grading and grade essay questions. When the grading is finished, the instructor can sync grades with the Learning Management system in Canvas for students to view. In addition, Remark provides built-in analysis reports that help quickly and efficiently analyze student performance.

Bulldog Central at Wingate University

Another very popular system that was launched by Wingate University and uses an AI bot is Bulldog Central. One part of the system allows the creation of a database with common questions and answers that students, staff, and instructors may have. When users come to the helpdesk section of Bulldog Central and start typing the questions or describing the issue they have, the bot matches the inquiry with the database of available information, and very often the user can get instant help and does not need to wait until somebody gets back with the answer.

Different areas of the university are working on adding more information to the knowledge database. The goal of Bulldog Central is to become a one-stop for students with all the basic generic questions that repeat often, to help them quickly and efficiently so they can focus on learning. Other specialists on campus can have more time to work on the special projects or issues when the bot will take care of the basic questions.

ARTIFICIAL INTELLIGENCE IN EDUCATION IN TEN YEARS (2032)

It is important to prepare students of today for the future. The International Society for Technology in Education (ISTE) is a leading organization that encourages educators to teach students to use technology to solve problems.

ISTE is providing six major standards for educators that encourage them to keep up with the constantly changing technology and adapt to it.

The main ISTE standards that education will follow in the near future are the following:

- Leverage technology to take an active role in choosing, achieving, and demonstrating competency in their learning goals, informed by learning sciences.
- Assist students to recognize the rights, responsibilities, and opportunities of living, learning, and working in an interconnected digital world.
- Curate a variety of resources using digital tools to construct knowledge, produce creative artifacts, and make meaningful learning experiences for themselves and others.
- Use a variety of technologies within a design process to identify and solve problems by creating new, useful, or imaginative solutions.
- Develop and employ strategies for understanding and solving problems in ways that leverage the power of technological methods to develop and test solutions.
- Communicate clearly and express oneself creatively for a variety of purposes using the platforms, tools, styles, formats, and digital media appropriate to their goals.
- Use digital tools to broaden their perspectives and enrich their learning by collaborating with others and working effectively in teams locally and globally. (ISTE, n.d.)

PricewaterhouseCoopers (PwC) in its report states that "in 10 years if you are not using some kind of AI-enhanced assistant, it will be like not being on the internet today" (Kaza Razat in PWC Bot.me booklet). Schools in the next 10 years have to model the application of AI to help students get familiar with AI and grow accustomed to using it as a tool in their work. The areas of education that have the potential to prepare students for the future of the AI world are STEM fields, project-based learning, design thinking, and storytelling (Zimmerman, 2018).

Educators are not sure what is better, to include in the curriculum addressing future AI needs or teaching students to code. Others argue that machines will be able to produce code faster than humans. It is important to be flexible. Some parts of the teaching profession may be replaced by machines like grading and providing basic knowledge lectures. However, there always will be a need for a teacher's role. Teachers will be freed to put more effort into what humans can do better, such as developing effective questioning strategies, transferring learning from one setting to another, and constructing knowledge (Zimmerman, 2018).

Design Thinking

Classrooms that use the design-thinking method are very structured and encourage creativity. Stanford University has a Design School that is focused on developing creativity in a variety of fields including K-12. This method can be applied to a variety of problems, which often are very complicated. The design-thinking method starts with navigating the ambiguity, which is the ability to recognize the discomfort of not knowing. The participants have to use creative thinking with some Design School tools to arrive at striking transformations.

The participants have to define the problem, propose ideas and develop prototypes that are followed by the phase of testing, feedback, and reflection. Design thinking is a very powerful method that changes how students think about themselves and their ability to impact the world. It emphasizes different ideas, and creativity, and will be crucial in the world of AI (Stanford d.school).

STEM

When seven leaders in STEM education were asked about what teachers need to focus on to prepare students for jobs of the future, they listed a mix of soft and traditional academic skills (Adams, 2017). One subject a student can use across different disciplines is statistics. It will help understand probability and error rates. The ability to solve problems will be very important in the future. Students maybe will not be using calculus problems, but the way it teaches students to think about problems will be useful in many situations. Encouraging students to think about a variety of possible solutions, and come up with different solutions, encourages creativity.

In math and science, students can be exposed to different models so they understand that there are different ways to solve problems. Students should be encouraged to participate in argumentation based on analytical thinking skills, looking for data patterns, explaining those data patterns, and building arguments to support their ideas. Workers of the future will need to do more than master the content. They need to be innovators and be able to ask questions that help build connections. They will need to be lifelong learners driven by intellectual curiosity.

Data-Based Decision-Making

To be successful in the future students should be able to make decisions based on scientific data and not on what they think or feel, regardless of their career. Teachers should build their curricula around authentic problems that students will work on and use different areas of their knowledge—statistics, technology, and programming systems—to communicate clearly and be flexible as the situation changes (Adams, 2017). For a long time, STEM was considered as learning the sciences, working on math problems, developing calculations, and not very related to creativity.

From STEM to STEAM

However, as time passes it is clear that art is very important in STEM sciences as each area of STEM incorporates art to some degree. Researchers show that brains will process information that is science and art related if they are exposed to it, and in the future will be able to demonstrate connections and solve complex problems. Many educators now add A to STEM, making it STEAM education as each engineer or mathematician has to think about the design first of all. Teaching students STEM in isolation will not prepare them for the future world of AI.

Gender Equality

The question of gender equality and diversity is important now and will be important in the future. Today, the tech industry and STEM are still dominated by men. As technology often develops exponentially, there will be more demand for careers related to science, technology, engineering, and math connected to art. It is important to teach students cultural diversity, encourage them to be respectful, and help them understand that STEM is for everyone. When it comes to gender, to help females thrive in technology fields, it is important to expose them to Lego, remote-controlled cars, board games, and help them believe that technology is for them.

Project-Based Learning

Project-based learning is a pedagogical method where a project is assigned to a team or a student to demonstrate learning through methods, such as video, posters, presentations, graphic design, and other media. Project-based learning does not replace traditional learning; it adds a new layer of creativity. Students have the opportunity to learn information in a more creative way versus pure memorization. Projects have a more complex structure in comparison to traditional assessments and require much planning and decision-making during the process of working on the project.

Students have to identify the problem and make plans for solving it. Students get experience in doing the research, defining the technology they will need, and applying the knowledge they gain to solve the problem.

Creativity is a big part of project-based learning. There may be several ways to complete the project and students get to choose the one they see as the best. Project-based learning has the potential to help students become better at what machines cannot do well—transferring knowledge from one domain to another (Zimmerman, 2018). Project-based learning is a method to prepare students for the world of AI (Garbade, 2021).

Storytelling and AI

Storytelling is a skill that can help students prepare for the work of the future. Storytelling does not seem to have much in common with STEM and computer science. Storytelling is a natural skill of humans. It is a way cultures pass wisdom to younger generations. A programmer can have an idea and develop it into life. He can tell a story using the coding language. This is the process machines cannot replicate. Machines cannot imagine and transfer knowledge from one domain into another. They do not have the natural intelligence that humans have (Zimmerman, 2018).

EDUCATORS' TASK AND PERSONALIZED LEARNING

Educators will have to be more knowledgeable about tools that help them work smarter, not harder. Many educators already know how to use video conferencing and learning management systems. After the COVID-19 pandemic, most every instructor learned how to use Zoom, Microsoft Teams, or other video conferencing tools to deliver basic instruction. Now they will have to learn to use the same tools to add social aspects to learning and bring more collaboration and communication options as students take courses remotely. Educators will have to work on learning how to pull all the systems together to deliver the best results.

Many AI-powered tools will be more available to offer the engines for content delivery, remediation, and review, for providing personalized pathways. Personalization will be on the rise in the next 10 years. No two students learn at the same pace. Learners differ in their understanding, culture, life circumstances, direction for the future, expectations, and the like. The process of education will be shifting more to the human element of education. It will be focused more on unique needs and differences learners possess to help them excel. AI is opening opportunities for new levels of personalization than ever existed before.

They help instructors better understand how each child learns and offers a tool to help students explore their curiosity (Zimmerman, 2018). Some educators still feel uncertain about personalized learning. They are not sure how students can learn what they need for a standardized test. There are several aspects of personalized learning instructors will have to understand and be able to incorporate into the learning process. Students should work as much as possible on real-world activities that match their interests and still meet the content standards required for the course.

Schools of the future will not be the only source of content for students. Educators should coach, support, and facilitate as students are working on the content watching, reading, and researching. Students should be encouraged to use critical thinking and creativity as they move toward their learning goals. Some students may choose to write a song about the system in the human body; others may choose to make a game or create a movie. Personalized learning gives educators more time and opportunities to guide students, intervene, and provide feedback as students practice autonomy, self-regulation, and personal decisions about their learning.

ARTIFICIAL INTELLIGENCE IN EDUCATION BY 2050

AI seems to go through cycles of development just like many processes, developments, and innovations. Many innovations seem very impressive. They promise to change the way people work, think, and do certain things, and then come periods of slowdown. Some educational ideas and theories fade away, and then come back under new circumstances. Something new comes to the spotlight and takes center stage. AI experiences winter periods when there is a lack of funding for research. Then some advancements in research and technology bring new ideas and AI takes off for a new spin of growth again (Grudin, 2017).

Scientists predict that AI will experience many periods of winter that get replaced with periods of exponential growth. Educators need to prepare students to have a long-term vision and not be discouraged. It is important to help develop skills that are uniquely human, like creativity and critical thinking and move away from teaching that is only focused on processing and memorization. AI is advancing very fast. The job market will be changing and students of the future have to be prepared to navigate it easily (Zimmerman, 2018). Education, in general, will have to reconsider its purpose and goals.

Next Generation Learning Challenges (NGLC) My Ways provides tools and practices to help support the education that will prepare students for the future world. The article says that education in the 2040s will be very different from today (NGLC My Ways, n.d.). The article shares the learning outcomes needed for the students of the future. It shares the results of research from My Ways, seven survival skills, goals for deeper learning, the

Collaborative for Academic Social and Emotional Learning (CASEL), and World Economic Forum's top ten skills (Ark, 2021).

Skills Needed for the Future

The top skills based on the research from all these organizations include critical thinking and problem solving, creativity and entrepreneurship, collaboration, emotional intelligence, decision-making, effective communication, agility and adaptability, initiative, and a positive mindset. In its report, PwC states that education will need a new definition of what it means to be smart, one that promotes higher levels of human thinking and emotional engagement (PWC, 2017). It will be important for schools to change the way learning and assessments are designed.

Ark (2021), suggests that educators should honor teaching methods that encourage deep creation and engagement, and avoid a plain content transfer. The human development of a student should be an integration of personal, social, and interdisciplinary knowledge. Educators should invite the community into the classroom. The insights of parents and community members are important to help build the community they want and connect with the available resources (Ark, 2021). Educators should have a mindset that anticipates change and focus on making adjustments and improvements to the learning process if life changes itself.

High Touch, High Tech

AI has great potential to bring more depth and quality to education in the next 30 years. Schools collect much information about students' performance and assessments. If teachers analyze data, they can provide early intervention and guidance to help students succeed. Data mining is a branch of computer science that uses AI to identify trends in data. Educators will be using data mining increasingly for student performance data to identify a student who needs help (Haigh, in Zimmerman, 2018).

At the same time, instructors can identify students' strong areas, suggest courses to take to develop natural talent, and identify special talents and skills that only special employers may look for. Humans have a natural psychological need for connectedness, a sense of choice, and a feeling of success. When those needs are met, people are more likely to persist when challenging times come (Grudin, in Zimmerman, 2018). When AI helps with more repetitive, data-based tasks, teachers will have more opportunities to work with students' psychological needs.

Teachers, unlike AI, can learn about the nuances of students' behavior and make decisions on how to motivate and guide students better (Zimmerman,

2018). Machines can help fill in the gaps in mathematics and other sciences when human instructors will fulfill psychological needs. Such high-touch, high-tech systems that use the best of AI and humans will gain much popularity in the future. AI has proven itself reliable in assessments. AI-powered assessments now can handle more complicated responses in addition to multiple choice answers.

Machines can now process human language, use machine vision, and learn with every answer. AI-powered assessments will be used widely in the future, which will help automate most of the assessment process and save time for instructors to work on more complicated tasks and tasks that machines cannot address. The future of education is in personalization. Systems similar to ALEKS will offer adaptive-learning programs for students. The program will be able to analyze how a student is doing and add more practice to fill in the learning gaps.

The Student Dashboard

Students will have a dashboard that shows the program, the level of mastery achieved, and the amount of work left. All the work in the course will be individually selected and adjusted based on the student's performance, learning objectives, and student goals. AI is a powerful engine behind the learning program to make personalization possible for each student. AI will also be used in physical education and sports to boost performance and health and avoid injuries.

AI will be used more to do post-game analysis and in-game performance. Coaches in schools will be regularly using AI-powered tools to help prepare athletes for their best performance. Schools will be using data from wearable technology to gain data to personalize training and diet, analyze athlete performance, biodynamics, talent identification, and selection (Rizzoli, 2022). Chatbots are another tool that will become very common in the next 30 years in education.

They can do several tasks and can be very time-saving for teachers. Chatbots can free up teachers by automating providing information to students. In addition to information retrieval, chatbots can provide transactional services by looking up information, doing and completing a transaction, advising by giving a suggestion based on the information available, and socializing by having a conversation with the learner (Zimmerman, 2018). Chatbots can be now created by instructors using the available tools. Teachers can already use several AI-enabled tools to help maximize the educational experience.

AI-Capable Tools

In the future, there will be more systems that include a variety of AI-capable tools that instructors can utilize easily. The technology will become easier and more intuitive to use in the next 30 years. The question that comes up often is that with all AI advances will the profession of a teacher still be around? Most educators who use AI are confident that the teaching profession still will continue. A variety of powerful AI tools only will help augment what teachers are doing. The hope in education is that AI will only help to do better with reading, writing, thinking, making decisions, creating, and innovating.

Teaching is not simply a transfer of knowledge. It requires deeper insight and making decisions about teaching methods and techniques. AI machines are not capable of such actions and always will have to be supplemented by humans. Machines will take part in the repetitive tasks of learning while teachers will focus on the human side of learning (Zimmerman, 2018).

CONCLUSION

AI is already a part of education and will be used even more in the future. AI-powered technologies show great benefits in education. Chatbots, data mining, and personalized learning management systems help free up instructors' time so they can focus on deeper topics, and work on special cases and projects with students. AI in education will help teachers achieve deeper, more meaningful educational results. Educators have to be very knowledgeable about AI-powered systems so they can engage them in classes easily. Educators of today have to think about preparing students for the future.

In that world, humans will be collaborating with AI-powered machines that can outperform humans in some areas and can teach themselves to improve their performance. At this point, most of the research points out that students of today will have to change and adapt their future careers depending on the impact of technology and AI on the future workforce. The top skills educators should be preparing students to have include critical thinking and problem solving, creativity and entrepreneurship, collaboration, emotional intelligence, decision-making, effective communication, agility and adaptability, initiative, and a positive mindset.

CHAPTER SUMMARIES

- Artificial intelligence (AI) is already present in schools in non-teaching as well as teaching aspects of education.

- The move to personalized learning with focus on the individual student differs from traditional learning approaches when everybody does one thing at the same time.
- Chatbots help instructors answer repetitive questions.
- When the student asks a question, the bot searches for a similar place in the video lectures and starts playing the video lecture from the moment that answers the question.
- A very popular system that was launched by Wingate University and uses an AI bot is Bulldog Central.
- Classrooms that use the design-thinking method are very structured and encourage creativity.
- To be successful in the future, students should be able to make decisions based on scientific data and not on what they think or feel, regardless of their career.
- When it comes to gender, to help females thrive in technology fields, it is important to expose them to Lego, remote-controlled cars, board games, and help them believe that technology is for them.
- Storytelling is a skill that can help students prepare for the work of the future.
- Students should be encouraged to use critical thinking and creativity as they move toward their learning goals.
- Educators need to prepare students to have a long-term vision and not be discouraged.
- The top skills based on the research from all these organizations include critical thinking and problem solving, creativity and entrepreneurship, collaboration, emotional intelligence, decision-making, effective communication, agility and adaptability, initiative, and a positive mindset.
- Schools in the next 10 years have to model the application of AI to help students get familiar with AI and grow accustomed to using it as a tool in their work.
- Design thinking is a very powerful method that changes how students think about themselves and their ability to impact the world.
- Project-based learning does not replace traditional learning; it adds a new layer of creativity.
- AI-powered assessments will be used widely in the future, which will help automate most of the assessment process and save time for instructors to work on more complicated tasks and tasks that machines cannot address.AI in education will help teachers achieve deeper, more meaningful educational results.

REFERENCES

Adams, Caralee on February 23, 2017 .contest-social .share-links svg. (2017, July 17). *The 7 most important stem skills we should be teaching our kids.* We Are Teachers. Retrieved June 30, 2022, from https://www.weareteachers.com/important-stem -skills-teaching-kids/

Ark, T. V. (2021, January 12). *Staying ahead of the robots: What grads should know and be able to do (opinion).* Education Week. Retrieved June 27, 2022, from https://www.edweek.org/teaching-learning/opinion-staying-ahead-of-the-robots -what-grads-should-know-and-be-able-to-do/2017/08

Falmagne, J.-C., Cosyn, E., Doignon, J.-P., & Thi´ery, N. (n.d.). *The assessment of knowledge, in theory and in practice.* Retrieved May 31, 2022, from https://www .aleks.com/about_aleks/Science_Behind_ALEKS.pdf

Garbade, D. M. J. (2021, August 11). *Artificial intelligence and the rise of project-based learning.* eLearning Industry. Retrieved July 6, 2022, from https://elearningindustry .com/artificial-intelligence-and-the-rise-of-project-based-learning

Getting Smart. (2017, July 13). *PWC report: AI boosts value of thinking, creativity and problem-solving.* Retrieved June 27, 2022, from https://www.gettingsmart .com/2017/07/13/pwc-report-ai-boosts-value-of-thinking-creativity-and-problem -solving/

Goel, A. (2017, November 6). *Ashok Goel - Jill Watson and friends: Virtual tutors for online education.* YouTube. Retrieved June 29, 2022, from https://www.youtube .com/watch?v=K-9qLZ2qdAk

Grudin, J. (2017). *Reinventing the right curriculum is impossible - but necessary!* THE Journal. Retrieved June 30, 2022, from https://thejournal.com/articles/2017 /04/17/reinventing-the-right-curriculum-is-impossible.aspx?admgarea=News1& %3Bm=2

ISTE. (n.d.). *ISTE standards: Students.* Retrieved July 6, 2022, from https://www.iste .org/standards/iste-standards-for-students

Manthorpe, R. (2019, September 21). *Artificial intelligence being used in schools to detect self-harm and bullying.* Sky News. Retrieved July 6, 2022, from https: //news.sky.com/story/artificial-intelligence-being-used-in-schools-to-detect-self -harm-and-bullying-11815865

NGLC. (n.d.). *MyWays.* Retrieved June 27, 2022, from https://myways.nextgenlearning .org/

PWC (n.d.). *Bot.me booklet.* Retrieved June 28, 2022, from https://www.pwc.com/us /en/industry/entertainment-media/publications/consumer-intelligence-series/assets /pwc-botme-booklet.pdf

Reiss, M. J. (2021, January 1). *Directory of open access journals.* London Review of Education. Retrieved July 6, 2022, from https://doaj.org/article/0fd8abb08d38400 99d43bd56dbf7389f

McGraw Hill ALEKS. (n.d.). *Research behind Aleks.* Retrieved July 6, 2022, from https://www.aleks.com/about_aleks/research_behind

Rizzoli, A. (2022, June). *7 game-changing AI applications in the sports industry.* V7. Retrieved July 5, 2022, from https://www.v7labs.com/blog/ai-in-sports#:~:text

=AI%20is%20used%20in%20sports,tactics%2C%20and%20maximize%20their %20strengths

Stanford d.school. (n.d.). *About*. Retrieved June 29, 2022, from https://dschool .stanford.edu/about

Zimmerman Michelle Renée. (2018). *Teaching AI: Exploring new frontiers for learning*. International Society for Technology in Education.

Chapter 3

Artificial Intelligence and Technical Programs

Shenika Ward and Darrel Staat

The Fourth Industrial Revolution is a way of describing the blurring of boundaries between the physical, digital, and biological worlds. It is a fusion of advancements in artificial intelligence (AI), robotics, the Internet of Things (IoT), 3D printing, genetic engineering, quantum computing, and other technologies (Schwab, 2016). This revolution is the collective force behind many products and services that are fast becoming indispensable to modern life.

Think about GPS systems that suggest the fastest route to a destination, voice-activated virtual assistants such as Apple's Siri, Google's Alexa, personalized Netflix recommendations, and Facebook's ability to recognize face and tag it in a friend's photo. As a result of this perfect storm of technologies, the Fourth Industrial Revolution is paving the way for transformative changes in the way life is lived and radically disrupting almost every higher education institution and business sector. This is all happening at an unprecedented, whirlwind pace.

Institutions of higher education have a responsibility to adapt to technology as advancements are made. Institutions of higher education must ensure that learners have the necessary skills they need to excel in their careers. Learners can benefit greatly from real-time, hands-on experiences. It is imperative that higher education leaders build meaningful relationships with industries. This is important for both present and future technical programming. Building these relationships are both beneficial to the community and the learners who will enter these roles within their respective industry.

AI, or intelligence demonstrated by machines as opposed to human beings, is one of the ways that Elon Musk has become a household name. Tesla, one of the first automobiles of its kind, offers its drivers a partially autonomous driving experience. This is made possible by the use of AI. The interesting thing about Tesla is that AI exists in so many other areas that are not necessarily recognized by the average human being. Elon Musk, along with his Tesla association, are more easily identified (Vance, 2015).

However, there are many instances in finance, transportation, defense and resource management that offer alternatives to human operation. While the average person may not think about the ways in which one's life is made easier by the scientists and programmers who create these life-changing operations, there are not many who can say they have not benefited in some way from AI.

Artificial Intelligence in Higher Education Today (2022)

In 2022, there are multiple platforms to name that are used daily by humans looking for ease in daily tasks or simply for entertainment. Network platforms are digital services that provide value to their users by aggregating those users in large numbers, often at a transnational and global scale (Kissinger et al., 2021). From social media to web searches, video streaming, ride-sharing, and more, there is a function for almost everyone. Each of these global platforms uses some aspect of AI. The good and sometimes bad things about these platforms are that they have the ability to deliver information quickly and are integrated in everyday life.

AI: ROBOTS AND TECHNICAL PROGRAMS IN HIGHER ED

Imagine having an employee who never gets sick, never needs a smoke or lunch break, and one who never runs the risk of needing to be out for an extended time due to maternity leave. This employee is always on time, never complains about workload, and can work in complete autonomy, with no supervision and little to no mistakes. There are not many human beings, if any, who meet this description. There is an object that can do all of these things; however, not in the form of a human being. AI involves a process of programming objects or systems to conduct operations similar to human beings.

The Use of Robots

The use of robots to perform some job functions allows corporations to perform better and faster, typically cutting processing time in half. Higher education institutions currently use robots in many technical programs. In community colleges, there are often more hands-on, technical programs where robots provide students with the opportunity to gain real-world experience without ever having to leave campus. This allows students the time to learn, while also allowing them to build their confidence along the way.

For instance, in many nursing programs across the nation, students have patients in the form of robots that they care for. These are very similar to actual human patients. AI has given students the opportunity to learn on campus in more practical ways. It allows the students to learn about dangerous situations without ever touching a human patient. These robots allow for more practical experience without having the student dealing with an actual patient in a hospital setting.

AI: Machine Learning and Technical Programs in Higher Ed

Machine learning, which is the process technology undergoes to acquire knowledge and capability often in significantly briefer time frames than human learning processes require, has been continually expanding into applications in medicine, environmental protection, transportation, law enforcement, defense, and other fields (Kissinger et al., 2021). AI is used in a multitude of areas to enhance performance for large and even small organizations. Machine learning and AI have both proven to be promising, and it is inevitable that education and training will be affected in some way or another.

Impact on Higher Education

Colleges and universities are already swimming in data, and there is much more on the way. Many institutions have already developed machine learning programs. Community colleges utilize continuing education courses and programs to train in the area of machine learning. More often than, not these programs are catered to the direct needs of the respective community college's workforce development needs. This is beneficial for students in need of training as well as the economic development of the community that surrounds the college. At the university level, graduate students can do research into the limits, if any, machine learning has.

AI: The Internet of Things and Technical Programs in Higher Ed

The IoT refers to applications such as high-speed networks, sensors, and automated processes. To a typical person, this sounds like a foreign language; however, what it translates to is faster processing, less buffering when streaming television shows, and enhanced experiences in virtual and augmented reality. Many of these processes have already come to fruition. These updates are the reason one may see less buffering when streaming shows or movies on popular streaming services as in previous years.

The ability to control one's thermostat or open their garage door from a location other than home, set security alarms, or unlock doors from a remote location are all examples of the IoT. There is no doubt that more processes will become easier and faster because of these innovations in technology through both AI and the IoT. The community college is unique in its approach to teaching and learning. There are significant differences in the way most colleges and universities operate as opposed to two-year community colleges.

Impact on Higher Education

Curriculum and continuing education vary in the ways they engage learners. In some instances, it appears that society views curriculum programs as more prestigious than learning a trade or enrolling in a technical school. In fact, technical programs, such as those teaching students to program machines, or to understand the behind the scenes of machine learning are in-demand fields that will prepare students for some of the premier jobs of the future. It will take continuous research into AI in order to understand what technologies are exponentially developing, which will need graduates with appropriate education and training to deal with them.

AI: 3D Printing and Technical Programs in Higher Ed

Grey's Anatomy, a television show that often has a futuristic vibe and is based on a hospital and various healthcare situations, was one of the first programs to highlight 3D printing. This technology might be one of the most significant to date. In the healthcare realm, 3D printing has the potential to transform the world of transplants among other things. Not only is there a significant impact on healthcare, but in manufacturing as well. The increase in use of 3D printing can be seen in various areas as there are endless opportunities to duplicate needed materials. One example is the number of masks suddenly needed during the Covid-19 epidemic.

Impact Higher Education

Higher education and technology are directly related. Both community colleges and universities alike will be directly affected by the changes. As higher education leaders, it is important to stay in the know about what new technologies are on the horizon. New technologies are emerging daily and will require colleges to adapt their programs and curricula to ensure they are prepared to educate learners who will either work in new fields or train the robots who will. There are several areas of particular interest that higher ed institutions will need to pay close attention to as they embrace the future.

They are AI, machine learning, robots, 3D printing, autonomous cars, and the IoT. Global network platforms may determine how colleges are marketed as well as how they cater to future learners both in and out of the classroom. Colleges should be on the front lines of machine learning as new technologies are realized, and colleges should be working with area industries to ensure the immediate needs of the community are met. Colleges must be forward-thinking about the healthcare possibilities that exist when 3D printing is more accessible.

The IoT is rapidly evolving and there is no doubt more advancements are on the way. Autonomous cars and trucks are being developed in the United States and around the world at a rapid rate. All of these technology enhancements that are on the horizon will likely come firing in one after the other in the form of disruptive technologies. Colleges and universities will need to think in a future-back method of planning in order to be prepared for what is to come (Johnson & Suskewicz, 2020).

To better understand the impact that AI will have in the future, it is important to know that AI technologies have the ability to see (computer vision), hear (speech recognition), and comprehend (natural language processing) now more than ever before.

Thirty years ago, there was not nearly as much data about healthcare, traffic, finance, and other important industries and topics so the possibilities of creating AI based solutions was not possible. With that in mind, it is safe to assume that ten years from now as new technologies begin to surface and become more powerful there will be access to even more data.

TECHNICAL PROGRAMS IN 2032

Artificial Technology and Machine Learning

The year 2032 has the potential to see significant changes in the technologies that will disrupt the current status of AI, machine learning, robots, 3D printing, autonomous cars, and the IoT. The reason for that disruption, good in this case, is that there will most likely be significant changes as each of these technologies develop exponentially, that is to say, not in a linear, step-by-step development over a long period of time, but in a method so rapid that it will seem to bring exponential change with little warning.

Quantum Computing

To begin with, AI is developing using quantum computing, which became a reality in September, 2019 with Google, followed closely by IBM, and other advanced computer researchers and engineers. Whereas the basis of computers then was transistors on silicon chips which, according to Moore's Law, double every 18–24 months, quantum computing uses atoms, which is so much faster that it makes Moore's Law look like it is going in reverse. The year 2032 will see both faster computing speed and increased computing storage that have created new normal in both categories.

The high-speed that quantum computing brings to the technical world will allow work to happen at velocities almost beyond comprehension. In turn, it gives machine learning a tremendous boost, which will increase the computer learning abilities at an exponentially high velocity. Scientists and engineers understand the possibilities, which is why in the United States the military through the Defense Advanced Research Projects Agency, (DARPA) is so interested in it (Jacobson, 2015). It also explains why China has developed a four million square foot facility to study the possibilities of quantum computing for military and non-military projects.

Further, according to futurist Ray Kurzweil, quantum computing makes it possible to create a computer brain, called a Singularity, which is equivalent in almost all areas to that of a human brain, with an IQ reaching toward 600 or more (Kurzweil, 2005). That is a truly frightening scenario. Some futurists see as the beginning of the end of the human race (Barrat, 2015). Other scientists see it as the beginning of truly amazing future for mankind (Friedman, 2017). Most likely it will take beyond 2032 to develop anything like a singularity, but the possibilities exist with quantum computing on the table.

Robots

As one thing leads to another, in 2032 AI is seriously collaborating with robots. Personal robots are serving businesses as receptionists, security, general maintenance, janitors, and lawn mowing to name a few. Those robots use minds supported by AI to do the various kinds of work at the business. In addition, personal robots are in the home providing cleaning services, security, meal preparation, grocery ordering, clothes washing, and other general household chores. They make housework for humans a thing of the past and they too have AI embedded in them directly or through a computer source in the home directing them.

Impact on Higher Education

Community colleges provide training to its students for algorithm development, robot repair and maintenance, and general robot problem solving. In addition, community colleges provide continuing education courses in how to manage a robot in the home and in the business. As newer robot models are developed, additional training for graduates and robot owners are provided to keep up with the ever-changing robot environment. Universities have developed courses and programs having to do with enhancing robots, creating operational algorithms, and addressing problems as they occur.

3D Printing

In 2032, most individuals and workplaces have 3D printers of various capacities as part of the home environment and the business facilities. 3D printing is a common in the home and business as personal computers were in the past decades. If something breaks or wears out in the household appliance, it is replaced by the needed object being produced in the home through 3D printing. The same is true for the business community where it is more efficient and financially less expensive to use the 3D printing than ordering the part from a distributor or local store. 3D printing is a commonly used method of producing parts.

Additive Manufacturing

Further, 3D printed houses, known as additive manufacturing, is a normal way to construct a house. It is much less expensive, constructed much more rapidly, and highly resistant to tornadoes, hurricanes, and other disruptive weather. Multi-story buildings such as apartments, condos, businesses, hospitals, factories, and warehouses are constructed in an additive manufactured method for the same reasons. The simplicity of the method makes it useful in a grand variety of areas, including rebuilding houses and other facilities following fire and flooding, or, extreme tornado and hurricane damage.

Beyond home and business use, additive manufacturing is used to construct car bodies, and parts for automobile engines made for fossil fuel use and those developed for electric power. Obviously, many things made of steel, aluminum, and fiberglass formerly using traditional methods are now created using additive manufacturing. Additive manufacturing makes considerable changes in a variety of industries across the board, including the ability to 3D print precise human organs used to replace those that are no longer useful. The year 2032 brings many improvements to everyday life.

At the higher education level there are new programs to instruct students as things change in daily life. It requires faculty with appropriate updated education and training, equipment to support the programs, and facilities of various sizes to house the programs. In addition, it created the need for more partnering with the business community in order to keep up with their ever-changing needs. In higher education there are new programs, additional equipment, and improved facilities. Research staffs at the college and university levels now work diligently to foresee what is coming and when the educational and training needs will appear.

Autonomous Cars and Trucks

In 2032, autonomous cars are owned and used by private individuals. The vehicles are very popular with senior citizens who no longer wish to drive or are unable to do so. Since the number of Americans over 70 years of age has increased very significantly due to longer lifespans, the need for the autonomous car has increased numerically in parallel with them. In addition, other individuals, resulting from sheer fascination about the car or not being interested in driving a car themselves, particularly in urban areas, own autonomous vehicles. A car that can drive itself is accepted as the new normal.

Historically, automobiles completely changed the transportation system for human beings in the early 20th century. They opened up the entire country to vacation travel, reconfigured urban areas to extensive suburban environments, created entirely new ways of living and types of work. In addition, the tractor, combines, and other gasoline powered farm machinery created wholesale changes in the agricultural world. Smaller farms of 160 acres soon became swallowed up in huge 500 to 5,000 acres farms, many that were owned by businesses rather than individual farmers.

Impact on the Business Community

Another other part of American society that moved to autonomous cars was the business community. Being taken from one place to another without a driver allowed work to be done during the travel time. In addition, autonomous trucks took over all long-range travel from city to city. At times, there is still the need an actual driver to take the truck from a distribution center to the final destination with the urban area, but there is research and design going on with trucks that will soon make movement from portal to portal a reality no matter the environment might be. As a capstone, the logistic system of moving goods and services reduces costs.

Autonomous vehicles brought many opportunities to the community college and university. Programs in repair and maintenance of autonomous cars and trucks are offered at the community college level. Autonomous vehicles provide the university with numerous research possibilities from developing algorithms to guide the car from point A to point B safely and securely, to designing logistical methods of transporting everything from individuals in cars to goods and services in the trucking industry. Further, in the near future there will be new programs as yet unthought of that will be needed at both levels of education.

The Internet of Things

By 2032, the IoT has become another normality within American and global societies. The tiny, inexpensive sensor is included in almost every manufactured item. Sensors that can tell when something is different or gone awry in a manufactured item ranging from a clothes washer to an automobile and send that information through the Internet to the cloud to build immense data bases of information that can be accessed by the manufacturer or other businesses. It has become part of the new normal. In fact, it is so normal that it is no longer questioned, but is only of concern when it does not operate correctly.

Hacking

The IoT is almost completely out of sight and mind, as it works its seeming magic behind the scenes. Hacking is still problem due to the use of quantum computing, which makes encryption of the data bases and sensors more complicated. There is research and design going on that will most likely take care of that problem by using quantum computing methods that are just recently being developed to make encryption as close to perfect as possible.

IoT provides the community college and the university with many education and training possibilities. Community colleges are offering certificates and associate degree programs needed to operate an IoT business. For those interested in researching the cloud for information on specific manufactured products and analyzing the outcomes of the research, a certificate or associate degree is a normal way to meet that need. On the university level considerable research is being done to develop methods of accessing the IoT clouds and using the information for the benefit of the business community.

TECHNICAL PROGRAMS IN 2050

Artificial Intelligence

AI has developed on a number of fronts. Healthcare has changed significantly. The study of genomes solved a number of health problems. Healthcare in 2050 is an extremely individualized process. Doctors, with the assistance of AI algorithms, are able to diagnose health issues, use appropriate procedures, and prescribe medications that are totally focused on the health issues of the individual. Therapies for diseases are personalized entirely so that the patient is treated as individually rather than as a case within group with a certain malady. Individualizing procedures, therapies, and medications improve a person's health tremendously.

Nanotechnology

Nanotechnology offers therapies that are injected into the blood stream that can attack the heath problems directly supporting the individualization of medical processes. Nanotechnology brings an entirely new way of working with patients in a variety health issues. It works in parallel with the body's natural defenses and helps the patient recover more quickly and completely. Further research in the 2050s most likely will also solve the aging process of the human body and allow for extended lifespans for everyone. The potential for nanotechnology in the medical field is phenomenal, a real game-changer (Dexler, 1987).

The Workplace

The workplace has changed tremendously in that the worker's productivity is improved continuously. Repetitive tasks handled by computer algorithms. Human are used for creative projects, complex problem solving, and work that cannot be accomplished by the computer (techvidvan.com). The workplace is flexible and interconnected globally. Computers and robots handle routine tasks while human workers provide the planning, interconnectedness, and imagination. Working collaboratively, the robot, the AI computer, and the human beings develop highly successful businesses that can rapidly adapt to changing conditions.

Artificial General Intelligence

Along with all the good results AI provides to the global economy and living standards, AI took machine learning to the extreme with the possibility of an AI that is equal to the human brain, including cognitive, creative, emotional, and thinking abilities. This is known as artificial general intelligence (AGI). And since there are no real limits on how far the AGI might be able to develop, in the near future there is the real possibility for AGI to increase significantly its IQ into the millions, and become an artificial super intelligence (ASI) that can think, create, imagine, and plan far beyond the known capabilities of the human mind.

AI and Robots

The AGI and ASI computer minds, when placed in the head of a robot directly or indirectly through connections to the Internet, has the potential to become the greatest assistant to the human race ever seen, and the most powerful negative being that humans have ever experienced. Some futurists believe that the rise of AGI and ASI means the end of human existence on earth (Barrat, 2013). Others believe that humans will become cyber-humans through implants (Barfield, 2013). In 2050, scientists, engineers, and national leaders are trying to figure out which way things may go and what they can do about it.

Impact on Higher Education

Education from kindergarten to graduate school and beyond will see amazing changes thanks to AI. The future of classrooms is digital. Education will become an individualized concept helping each student by starting where they are when they enter the classroom or online course and taking them to the goal set by the course no matter what the time and methods involved happen to be. AI assists with the planning, instruction, and evaluation of each student individually.

3D Printing or Additive Manufacturing

The Construction Industry

The construction industry in housing uses additive manufacturing for over 50% of new homes. Entire subdivisions across the United States, Europe, Asia, China, Australia, and India have been constructed during the past decade. House construction is less expensive, more rapid to build, and much stronger to the point that it can endure tornadoes and hurricanes with relatively little damage. Further, materials used for additive manufacturing vary tremendously from country to country. Additive manufacturing has also been used to replace traditionally built homes and business facilities following hurricanes in a matter of weeks instead of years.

The Health Industry

Physical organs for human beings, ranging from livers to hearts, are now created using 3D printing techniques. The organs have proven to work extremely well and last longer than those they replace. An entire medical industry has developed to supply the replacement needs of human beings. Just as other medical procedures have become totally individualized, so do 3D printed organs. They work so well because they are produced using sample cells from the person who is being treated. The entire medical industry creates what would be been thought of as magic just a few decades ago.

The Automotive Industry

Of course, the automotive industry has benefitted tremendously from the use of additive manufacturing. Complete car bodies can be created with options that are desired by the purchaser. It is now hard to tell what year a car was constructed because of the many individualized options available to the buyer. In addition, propulsion parts can be easily and much less expensively created than ever before. If something breaks or wears out, it can be easily replaced by the car dealership, or by the owners with their 3D printing processes at their homes. 3D printing in the automotive field is a normal part of everyday life.

Use in Space

Another interesting use of additive manufacturing is now being used on the moon that circles earth and Mars, the planet closest to the earth. As human beings now begin to inhabit these two planets, 3D printing, using local materials, are being used to construct housing and other facilities, again with the ability to withstand the changes in temperature on the moon and the sandstorms that are quite common on Mars. This allows for more exploration of the planets and living conditions that are satisfactory. It is expected that towns and even cities will soon be located on Mars, with additive manufacturing supplying the foundation for it all.

Impact on Education

Schools, such as existed in past decades, have either disappeared completely or have adapted to the latest business developments. Most schools are connected to or part of larger business entities. This allows for the firm to have a continuous incoming flow of educated and trained employees who will work for the company for a 3–5-year period before moving on to other job pursuits within the business or externally. Great emphasis is placed on individualized instruction from the elementary grade on up. Individuals are taught how to learn using various AI-developed methods from the time they begin their education until they retire in their nineties.

Robots for Manufacturing

Manufacturing robots are now the linchpins in the industry. They provide the processes needed for planning the product, constructing the product, packaging the product, loading it onto the appropriate delivery transportation and at the destination, and unloading and stacking the product appropriately. Algorithms direct the robots using machine learning techniques that allow the robots to develop from its original abilities and enabling it to complete tasks that were beyond its capabilities when constructed. The learning ability assists the robot to do its work more efficiently and increases the company's bottom line at the same time.

Personal Robots

Personal robots are normal parts of the household providing many mundane chores such as house cleaning, grocery shopping, and meal preparation, as well as providing security and comprehensive planning for humans from attending local events to taking expansive trips within the country and beyond. On more lengthy trips or vacations, the robots accompany the humans, providing a variety of services from obtaining tickets to events to cleaning up the rooms after the humans leave. The more sophisticated robots can select appropriate clothing, provide hair dressing, select shoes, and in general do what needs to be done.

Robots and Children

Personal robots are everywhere working with and assisting humans in a variety of ways families have robots for adults and for children. Robots assist children with their education from the earliest time they are able to learn on through their teenage years and more. When a son or daughter goes off to a residential college, their personal robot accompanies them. If the child decides on an online higher education, the robot is there to assist with research, editing of written work, and critiquing of artist abilities. Humans in 2050 probably wonder how things ever got done in the time before robots were ubiquitous.

Higher Education

Education is provided for the most part by robots in the classroom, lab, and at home. It is normal for teaching robots to work with children as they grow older. The robot knows what abilities and information needs be learned as the child grow older and provides the service in a most caring manner starting with children where they are and helping them through a variety of methods to learn what is appropriate year by year. Higher education is focused on learning how to learn in an exponentially changing, digital world. Students learn how to work in teams as well as on their own obtaining skills, capabilities, and knowledge needed for successful careers.

Fears Concerning Robots

Some adults in particular wonder if at some point the robots will become intelligent enough to literally take over everything. However, in 2050, that point is still far out in the future, if it will ever happen at all. Robots are initially programmed as assistants to help humans grow and develop. The federal governments have worked hard to make sure that the most important beings in the world are humans. Robots exist to help, encourage, and assist the human race, not the other way around. So far, that process has worked very well, and it is expected to continue far into the future, most likely for as long as the planet Earth exists.

Autonomous Vehicles

Autonomous cars, trucks, and motorcycles are only vehicles allowed on the streets, roads, and highways in the United States. The self-driven vehicle became illegal to be operated on streets, roads, and highways in 2045. There are still self-driven racing cars and trucks on fully enclosed race tracks. NASCAR still exists with a great following. Accidents do happen on the race track, but the number of accidents of autonomous vehicles have dropped to almost nothing. Those that do happen, very occasionally, are usually due to design flaws in the vehicles when produced. These are removed and upgraded or disposed of quickly and efficiently.

Travel in Autonomous Vehicles

Travel in autonomous vehicles is safer than ever before. In addition, they collaborate in groups like a train on long distance travel, which allows them to run at higher speeds than previously when individuals were driving. It also provides better mileage per kilowatt than before. There are no fossil-fueled vehicles on the road; they were outlawed a decade ago. All autonomous vehicles are electrically powered with electricity derived from wind and sun power; consequently, the climate issues of the 2020s are largely solved. Electrically powered, autonomous cars, trucks, and motorcycles now provide the transportation for human beings.

Impact on Higher Education

Education needed for autonomous vehicles are now provided by community colleges that are directly connected to manufacturing facilities, which allows for a smooth transition for students from high schools to learning centers in the manufacturing facilities. Universities also work directly with vehicle manufacturing facilities helping them to develop ever more efficient, effective, and artistically beautiful cars, trucks, and motorcycles. Currently, the transportation vehicle industries together with the universities are working to develop autonomous vehicles that will create their own electrical power through small, flat sun receptors mounted on the roof.

The Internet of Things

In 2050 the IoT is old hat. There are sensors relaying information to the cloud from almost manufactured item. Information from the sensors is ever-increasing on one hand and almost completely unseen or sensed on the other. Autonomous vehicles, robots, additive manufacturing, 3D printing, AI, and more are using the IoT in such a grand variety of ways that the only time IoT is even thought about happens when power operating the objects goes off for a period of time. Otherwise, if everything is running in a normal fashion, IoT is invisible, behind the scenes, and unnoticed.

No one in the 2050 decade thinks about or cares about the multitude of sensors surround them in appliances, robots, cars, trucks, clothing, houses, and cities. They exist everywhere and provide assistance to law enforcement, health organizations, medical procedures, the workforce, robots, homeowners, and a list that goes on and on. IoT is like electricity; everyone knows it is there, but no one gives it much thought. The IoT has blended into totally into everyday life and is accepted as normal. IoT has become a normal part of the world of education from kindergarten to graduate schools and everything in between.

Impact on Higher Education

Educational institutions have developed entire associate and bachelor degrees around the IoT. The IoT is the basis of jobs and industries for those interested in accessing the clouds, downloading, or analyzing information. Many occupations are IoT driven. The stock market sees IoT businesses as an extremely important segment of the industrial world. New ways to use IoT are developed on a daily basis as data is the bloodstream of everything from the banking industry to health organizations. Universities send their graduates into the working world that is clambering for those who understand on how to use IoT.

CONCLUSION

The year 2050 is an interesting world supported on every hand with existing technology and more developing on a daily basis. Keeping abreast with what is going on is a never-ending proposition. Nothing remains the same; everything changes continuously. The development of technology provides strong support for the Greek notion that the only absolute in the universe is change. It is most difficult to imagine what life and technology will be like by the year 2100.

CHAPTER SUMMARIES

- Institutions of higher learning have a responsibility to adapt to technology as advancements are made.
- From social media to web searches, video streaming, ride-sharing and more, there is a function for almost everyone.
- Higher education institutions currently use robots in many technical programs.
- The Internet of Things or "IoT" refers to applications such as high-speed networks, sensors, and automated processes.
- Colleges should be on the front lines of machine learning as new technologies are realized, and colleges should be working with area industries to ensure the immediate needs of the community are met.
- 2032 has the potential to see significant changes in the technologies that will disrupt the current status of AI, machine learning, robots, 3D printing, autonomous cars, and the IoT.
- 3D-printed houses, known as additive manufacturing, is a normal way to construct a house. It is much less expensive, constructed much more rapidly, and highly resistant to tornadoes, hurricanes, and other disruptive weather.
- Autonomous vehicles brought many opportunities to the community college and university. Programs in repair and maintenance of autonomous cars and trucks are offered at the community college level.

- Physical organs for human beings, ranging from livers to hearts, are now created using 3D-printing techniques.
- Robots assist children with their education from the earliest time they are able to learn on through their teenage years and more.

REFERENCES

Barfield, W. (2013). *Cyber-humans: Our future with machines.* Switzerland: Springer International Publishing.

Barrat, J. (2015). *Our final invention: Artificial intelligence and the end of the human era.* New York, NY: Thomas Dunne Books.

Dexler, K. (1987). *Engines of creation: The coming era of nanotechnology.* New York, NY: Anchor Books, Division of Random House.

Friedman, T. (2017). *Thank you for being late: An optimist's guide to thriving in the age of accelerations.* New York, NY: Picador, MacMillan Publishing Group, LLC.

Jacobson, A. (2015). *The pentagon's brain: An uncensored history of DARPA, America's top secret military research agency.* New York, NY: Little, Brown and Company.

Johnson, M & Suskewicz, J. (2020). *Lead from the future: How to turn visionary thinking into breakthough growth.* Boston, MA: Harvard Business Review.

Kissinger, H, Schmit, E, & Huttenlocher, D. (2021). *The age of AI and our human future.* New York, NY: Little, Brown, and Company.

Kurzweil, R. (2005). *The singularity is near: When humans transcend biology.* London, England: Penguin Books Ltd.

Schwab, K. (2016). *The fourth industrial revolution.* Geneva Switzerland: World Economic Forum.

Vance, A. (2015). *Elon Musk: Tesla, Space x, and the quest for a fantastic future.* New York, NY: HarperCollins Publisher.

Chapter 4

Artificial Intelligence and Student Affairs

Demetria Smith

Artificial intelligence (AI) has been significantly integrated in day-to-day life over the past several decades. In the simplest of terms, AI can be defined as "the attempt to create machines that can do things previously possible only through human cognition" (Zeide, 2019). AI can be seen throughout prominent areas of society. This includes innovative agricultural land navigation, life-saving medical operations, contemporary communication, and the dissemination of education. Higher education is no exception to the uptick in AI usage in contemporary society.

STUDENT AFFAIRS

While the immediate assumption of AI in higher education is likely in educational and instructional practices, student affairs has also seen a tremendous increase in the usage of AI over the last several years. Student affairs is most simply defined as all of the departments, offices, and personnel that support learners outside of the classroom at colleges and universities. This includes, but is not limited to admissions, student engagement, leadership development, academic resources, disabilities services, and many other areas.

Student affairs professionals today have discovered innovative methods of incorporating AI into higher education. In addition to the usages of AI within contemporary student affairs, technologists, and student affairs administrators are not resting on what currently works. They are consistently looking at new ways to incorporate AI and technology into student affairs to provide the best possible support for learners at postsecondary institutions. Many of today's

AI implementations have the ability to be expanded and that could potentially be evident in the near future.

AI AND STUDENT AFFAIRS IN 2022

Humans have been utilizing AI heavily within modern society, oftentimes without even noticing that it is integrated in the simplest of daily tasks. Precise voice recognition/translation in GPS systems, facial recognition on social media applications, and listening or reading suggestions from Amazon and Spotify are all examples of AI used on a regular basis (Zeide, 2019). Similar tools and technological techniques are used within student affairs and higher education for the benefit of contemporary learners.

Institutional Application

Today, colleges and universities "increasingly rely on algorithms for marketing to prospective students, estimating class size, planning curricula, and allocating resources such as financial aid and facilities" (Zeide, 2019). Admissions and enrollment officers have extended their use of social media algorithms for targeted ads and marketing to prospective students. This provides increased visibility for institutions on platforms where the majority of prospective students can be found. AI can also support enrollment efforts.

For example, Georgia State University has found success in using Pounce, a chatbot that makes contact with students who have not completed certain tasks by their respective deadlines. This has reduced the *summer melt* by 20%. Pounce has assisted Georgia State University increase equity for students that may be at higher risk for lack of completion by providing an additional tool to support retention. In addition, algorithms can analyze course objectives and expected outcomes in order to assist instructors in planning curricula and identifying resources aligned with the content being taught in any particular course.

Present Benefits

Higher educational institutions have already seen several benefits of using AI in institutional application. Colleges and universities are able to extend their outreach to students as well through targeted marketing. There is currently a significant decline in enrollment, matriculation, and retention of students within higher education, so the benefits of targeted marketing could be immeasurable. AI can be used to contest declining trends and mitigate several of these concerns (Barrett, et al., 2019). Colleges and universities are also able to save money on traveling to admissions fairs and events.

Having the ability to promote the institution without having to physically attend recruitment fairs or visit schools that are distant from the institution can save money on transportation, vehicles, gas, mileage, and meals. Finally, more attention can be paid to intentionality when developing or modernizing curricula. This can produce more relevant programs of study to best suit the occupations and industries of the future.

Present Drawbacks

Of course, with benefits of utilizing AI in student affairs, there are also some drawbacks. Utilizing targeted marketing and doing less face-to-face recruitment minimizes some of the personalized touches in initial interactions with prospective students. Modern students want to ensure they are making sound investments and that they are able to get the most out of pursuing higher education. Many institutions are targeting the same demographic of prospective students, so admissions officers must do whatever it takes to make the institution and the admissions process stand out from others.

Student Support

Student support is another area of student affairs where AI is applied in such areas as academic advising and guidance. Offices and departments of academic and career advising use AI systems for scheduling, course recommendations, and even assisting students in navigating career paths. These tools, and those similar to them, maintain and archive the performance of past students in order to make recommendations for future students. "For students who are struggling with chemistry, the tools may steer them away from a pre-med major, or they may suggest data visualization to a visual artist" (Zeide, 2019).

This is a very popular use of AI in student affairs and is presently implemented at numerous colleges and universities across the globe. At Elon University, AI is used to track courses a student has taken previously and assists them apply that information to planning for future course enrollments (Gardner, 2018). Financial aid is also an area where AI is presently being applied. Colleges and universities can provide *just-in-time* financial aid solutions for students that may need last minute funds to remain enrolled.

They also provide early intervention for students across numerous areas, to include nonacademic, academic, and operational needs (Zeide, 2019). If students find themselves delayed on financial aid, behind in submitting enrollment documents, failing coursework, or needing maintenance in residential living, all of these can be addressed through predictive analytics supported through AI.

Student affairs is not frequently staffed as effectively as it could be to provide the greatest level of supports for students. This is usually due to budgetary limitations. By relying on AI to handle several of the tasks involved in student affairs, the demand to meet the immediate and future needs of students is better addressed. Students are able to receive the support they need academically, personally, and professionally in real time versus having to schedule appointments. This is also beneficial for students with lower levels of English comprehension or English not being the students' primary language.

AI can provide support and guidance from student affairs to students in their respective native languages. This will increase the likelihood of these students being able to have equitable access to student supports. In addition, support for students is timelier. AI systems can use much more granular patterns of information and student behavior for real time, up-to-the-minute assessment of student risk (Zeide, 2019). Being able to provide support in real time can address multiple student needs in a more time-efficient manner than what can be done with humans alone.

Importance of Relationships

A significant component of the student experience is the ability to connect and build community while enrolled at an institution of higher education. Admissions counselors build initial relationships with students, and orientation coordinators see them through early student programming and into enrollment and starting classes. Success counselors and advisors support students throughout their time enrolled, while student engagement administrators help students to connect with other students to build community.

With AI handling many of these tasks, students do not have as much opportunity to connect to campus officials and develop those essential campus connections. Also, some at-risk students require that personalized touch and require human interaction in order for the interventions to be successful. Having more AI respond to and apply these interventions could have a negative impact on students engaging with the institution, which could ultimately lead to them leaving the institution or dropping out of school altogether.

INSTRUCTIONAL APPLICATION

The final application of AI within higher education is not as directly correlated with student affairs, but student affairs plays a major role in supporting it. Instructional application involves developing systems that are able to respond to student needs, progression, and pace. Personalized learning systems are able to analyze student progress in real time and make recommendations to administrators and faculty on performance.

This is particularly useful for success counselors and disabilities services professionals, as they are able to use these recommendations to determine where they can incorporate additional supports or accommodations are necessary for any particular student. Students can also monitor and set their own pace and progress with AI systems for instructional application. Self-paced progress gives students a higher level of autonomy and ownership of their education, which benefits their likelihood to progress through to matriculation.

Degree Completion

The ultimate goal of enrolling at any institution of higher education should be matriculation or completion of a degree, specialization, or certification. Instructional application of AI is an effective method of providing the necessary resources for students to progress and matriculate. Student affairs professionals are able to use the data extracted from these systems to provide the support needed to student throughout the duration of their enrollment at any given institution.

They can also alert faculty members and instructors of any student progression concerns to which they have been alerted, giving instructors better opportunity to incorporate their own forms of interventions and supports to help students that may get off track.

Present Drawbacks

There is one major drawback to instructional application of AI. These machines and systems cannot yet effectively process human response to circumstances and how those circumstances may impact performance and progress. For example, if a nontraditional student loses their job in the middle of a term, there could be emotional and financial impacts from that. The student may focus more on finding a new job and providing for their family that educational progression becomes an afterthought. AI does not have the ability to consider this; instead, systems only see that the student is falling behind and sends alerts.

These alerts of poor performance and lack of progress could add more stress and frustration to the student, potentially causing them to withdraw, drop out, or fail coursework. While AI may dominate efficiency and performance, it simply does not have the capacity to match human compassion and empathy.

AI AND STUDENT AFFAIRS IN 2032

As time progresses, society can expect to continually see AI improve its ability to interpret more intricate patterns. AI is evident in virtually every aspect of contemporary life, and there are no signs of that slowing down within the next decade. Higher education is not exempt from integration with this, by any means. Technological advancements and increased usage of AI have the potential to derive both positive and negative effects on aspects of higher education. Elana Zeide (2019) highlights the fact that society is not at the point where there may be some forms of humanoid instructors managing classes.

She notes that there are a few physical attributes, specifically referring to the IoT, where sensors are able to collect data from sensory sources (Zeide, 2019). However, the AI of 2022 is still primarily housed in two-dimensional software-processing systems. This could likely change drastically by 2032. Susan Fourtane (2021) analyzed the role of AI in the future of higher education and emphasized the notion of AI becoming the norm in all aspects of higher education, including student affairs.

By 2032, the major applications of AI in student affairs will expand and diversify exceptionally. For example, student affairs professionals can utilize AI to manage the data that is shared and how students can access it. By 2032, students will surpass using secure portals and passwords and rather use facial recognition and other forms of biotechnology to further protect data. Colleges and universities will be able to better engage their alumni through more specific targeting to events, fundraisers, and opportunities that align with their specific careers, industries, and interests.

Improvements in Student Services Efficiency

Several institutions of higher education are looking at ways to improve student services efficiency and technology has been a significant tool incorporated into these improvements. There are now automated systems for registration, allowing quicker registrations without the requirement of traditional input by an academic advisor. By 2032, bots and AI may be able to evaluate transcripts and automatically generate schedules based on student profiles and degree progression worksheets. AI and exponential technologies have the ability to simplify, expedite, and improve processes across the realm of higher education.

With colleges and universities becoming more student-centered and committing to greater customer service, the incorporation of technology will be instrumental for the future of higher education. Student services will be able to expedite processes such as registration, financial aid processing, and academic interventions. Students will be able to get the supports and assistance they need without limitations of human functioning such as scheduling/work hours, availability, and difficult personality types. With more efficient processes, more students can receive better service in less time boosting student admission, enrollment, and matriculation.

Digital Avatars and Building Community

Many colleges and universities are beginning to use chatbots and other forms of AI to communicate with and engage students from application and admission to enrollment and matriculation. Within the next 10 years, higher education administrators can expect to see major changes in how digital communication is done. Dr. Keith Whitfield, president of the University of Nevada-Las Vegas, provided a digital likeness of himself to be evolved into a chatbot. The purpose was to develop comfortability amongst students and make them feel included in the UNLV community.

While Whitfield is one of the first to incorporate a personal avatar as the institution's chatbot, within the next decade, other institutions will take on similar usage of AI on their campuses in order to better engage students. Success coaches could use avatars for students to build confidence in seeking them out as resources to acclimate to campus life, while financial aid counselors could use the same AI to provide a more interactive virtual experience with students that are attempting to navigate the financial aid process.

Supporting the Leaders of the Future

The occupations and industries of the future are presently being created, and it is likely that even more career paths will rely on AI within the next decade. Fourtane (2021) emphasizes the importance of all students needing to be provided with specific instruction on technical skills that will make them competent with programming and interacting with future AI. This may change what general education courses and prerequisites look like in higher education. However, it will still be vital to have skills that will support more critical soft skills.

This will drive change in how student affairs professionals prepare students for leadership outside of the classroom. There will be an increased need for student affairs professionals to create opportunities for students to develop these skills. For example, staff of an Office of Student Engagement may lead required co-curricular programming that focuses on defining emotional intelligence and how it applies to personal and professional growth. Involvement may become a requirement at universities to assist students in becoming more proficient with skills that require applying critical thinking, empathy, and grounded decision-making (Cliburn 2022).

Tutoring and Academic Resources

A key component of student affairs is academic resources or tutoring and academic support. Currently, several institutions offer a dedicated office or department in student affairs that provide academic support for students that may be struggling or off progression track in their courses. These resources include tutoring, disabilities services, accommodations management, and writing labs. Most of these offices and departments have minimal AI incorporated in them presently, as to provide services based on what a student has as a present need.

However, by 2032, that has a high likelihood of changing completely. Student affairs will be able to increase the ability to support students by using virtual reality and other forms of adaptive learning systems in order to provide more individualized learning resources for students. Tutoring may be more customizable to eventually include language translation, assessment of present level of understanding, and flexible hours of availability.

Improvement of Institutional Bottom Line & Reputation

According to Wiley University Contributors (2022), if an institution of higher education is able to identify and target specific applicants that are deemed an ideal fit for the school and personalize as many of the experiences throughout their enrollment, schools will be able to not only run more efficiently, but also offer a more worthwhile experience and enroll more students with higher likelihoods of matriculation. Timeliness is essential within student affairs and higher education. If a college or university is able to provide a positive experience for its students through avoidance of long wait times or processes, they will see a boost in reputational value.

Student affairs professionals, especially those who serve in the recruitment and admissions areas, can boast to potential students that the institution is equipped to support them effectively and efficiently, with personalized attention to an individual student's needs. With enrollment numbers being a major concern, AI may be the factor that shifts these trends within the 2030s and beyond.

AI AND STUDENT AFFAIRS IN 2050

There are limitless possibilities for how student affairs and higher education, in general, may be using AI by the midcentury. Systems will continue to advance and provide opportunity for unique integration into student affairs, from modest to the most intricate of tasks. Teaching and instruction will be more heavily impacted by AI in the midcentury than it is presently, and student affairs most certainly will.

Facial Recognition

While several industries have tapped into employing facial recognition to assist in operation, student affairs has not necessarily had the opportunity to do so in a way that does not violate student privacy but still is effective in improving student outcomes. Facial recognition could provide an opportunity for colleges and universities to provide state-of-the-art mental health services to students through detecting shifts in mood and emotion. Emotional analysis can be used for departments of Counseling and Wellness Services to support students in mental health crises.

Facial recognition used for Counseling and Wellness Services could provide more efficient care that is timely in nature by interpreting emotions and feelings through facial indicators. This could provide earlier interventions for students at postsecondary institutions that are at risk or in the midst of a mental health crisis. Potentially, the facial recognition software could send a notification to the health, wellness, or counseling center on campus that a student is in crisis (Zharovskikh, 2020).

More Effective Recruitment and Admissions Practices

Timing is essential in admissions and recruitment within higher education, and by 2050, AI can revolutionize the practices and processes of recruiting and admitting students. Algorithms will become more advanced and allow recruiting teams to focus more on developing and monitoring the algorithms versus actually completing domestic and international travel, saving time and money. In fact, the algorithms could also identify which enrolled students have the highest likelihood of progressing, matriculating, and serving as alumni that still engage with the institution at some level (Wiley University Contributors, 2022).

AI will also be able to personalize the admissions and enrollment process to best fit the needs of individual learners. One student may require visa processing, housing, and athletic scholarship approval, while another may only need course registration and a parking permit. Having the ability to customize each individual administrative admissions process gives admissions and enrollment officers the flexibility to only need to address any issues and verify that processes are completing, which may also likely be able to be handled by AI in the midcentury.

Impact on Institutional Employment, Strategic Planning, and Sustainability

Microsoft Research and Times Higher Education conducted a survey amongst global leaders to assess the benefits of the integration of AI in higher education. That survey acknowledged that AI will impact the future of employing qualified student affairs professionals, developing strategic long-range plans, and enforcing sustainability plans at colleges and universities. AI will be able to provide assessment and feedback to students as well as humans can, and faculty/staff positions will not be cut, but potentially expanded.

By midcentury, all institutions will not only have a strategic plan and AI plan, but also be actively implementing those plans. Universities will continue to provide training and learning opportunities for AI staff research most effectively. There will be major increase in the number of staff who will show interest in it. This also includes potentially getting other student affairs professionals interested. Postsecondary educational opportunities will be more in demand than ever in 2050. The demand for graduates in the fields of information technology and data analytics will be increasingly high.

Concerns, Considerations, and Ethics

There are already several concerns for how AI may impact humans and society, and those concerns will continually grow and likely become more prevalent in the midcentury.

Comprehensiveness of Data

In order for AI systems to be able to process information, data must first be input into them. Without the most diverse variety of data possible being input into the systems, there will always be a higher margin of error. In a survey conducted on facial recognition tools, it was found that facial recognition software and tools were more accurate for lighter-skinned people than darker-skinned people, noting almost 100% accuracy for light-skinned men and roughly 65% accuracy for dark-skinned women (Buolamwini & Gebru, 2018). This could be problematic if facial recognition becomes more heavily utilized within higher education.

Bias in Data and Algorithms

Similar to issues like comprehensiveness, biases in algorithms can be a major concern with AI in student affairs. Algorithms are not necessarily biased intentionally, but they are based on preexisting information that could have a biased result. If a college or university is developing targeted ads and marketing based on zip code, there may be issues with the types of advertisements that are displayed in the area. Some potential students could miss targeted marketing and could possibly make assumptions that the institution has no interest in their demographic.

Integrity of Relationships and Community Building

AI has already consumed so much of human processing, operation, and task execution. By 2050, it is likely that humans will witness even more integration of AI into society. It calls to question how much integrity will remain in building relationships and community, more specifically within institutions of higher education. Student affairs professionals constantly strive to ensure students feel connected to the institution and to develop genuine relationships throughout the duration of their time enrolled and even thereafter as alumni.

However, with so many opportunities for human interaction being replaced by AI for the benefit of efficiency, many may wonder if genuine relationships can actually be created and maintained. If students are more often interacting with chatbots or humanoid systems to support their success at colleges and universities, are they genuinely creating campus connections or are they connecting with technology? This is an issue that will undoubtedly be addressed the student affairs environment.

CONCLUSION

When evaluating AI's insertion in the realm of higher education, research notes that the size of AI within the education market surpassed $2 billion in 2021 and will likely continue to grow at a compound annual rate of over 45% between 2022 and 2030 (Global Market Insights, 2022). As the needs, desires, and expectations of learners continue to evolve and become increasingly demanding, it is vital that institutions of higher education are able to meet and exceed these demands. AI has already made significant impact within higher education and will continue to do so in both the near and distance future.

It will be imperative that educational administrators consider benefits and drawbacks of the implementation of AI within student affairs to determine what would work best for their respective institutions and learners. Regardless of whether the college or university incorporates substantial or minimal amounts of AI into student affairs administration, it is certain that campus communities will see some level of impact.

CHAPTER SUMMARIES

- Student affairs professionals today have discovered innovative methods of incorporating AI into higher education.
- Admissions and enrollment officers have extended their use of social media algorithms for targeted ads and marketing to prospective students.
- Financial aid is also an area where AI is presently being applied.
- AI can provide support and guidance from student affairs to students in their respective native languages.
- While AI may dominate efficiency and performance, it simply does not have the capacity to match human compassion and empathy.
- By 2032, the major applications of AI in student affairs will expand and diversify exceptionally.
- The occupations and industries of the future are presently being created, and it is likely that even more career paths will rely on AI within the next decade.
- With colleges and universities becoming more student-centered and committing to greater customer service, the incorporation of technology will be instrumental for the future of higher education.
- If a college or university is able to provide a positive experience for its students through avoidance of long wait times or processes, they will see a boost in reputational value.
- Facial recognition could provide an opportunity for colleges and universities to provide state-of-the-art mental health services to students through detecting shifts in mood and emotion.
- Algorithms will become more advanced and allow recruiting teams to focus more on developing and monitoring the algorithms versus actually completing domestic and international travel, saving time and money.
- By 2050, it is likely that humans will witness even more integration of AI into society.

REFERENCES

Barrett, M., Branson, L., Carter, S., DeLoan, F., Ellis, J., Gundlach, C., & Lee, D. (2019). Using artificial intelligence to enhance educational opportunities and student services in higher education. *Inquiry: The Journal of the Virginia Community Colleges, 22*(1). Retrieved from https://commons.vccs.edu/inquiry/vol22/iss1/11

Buolamnwini, J. & Gebru, T. (2018). Gender shades: Intersectional accuracy disparities in commercial gender classification. *Proceedings of Machine Learning Research, 81.*

Cliburn, E. (2022). *Universities embrace artificial intelligence to support students.* INSIGHT into Diversity. Retrieved from https://www.insightintodiversity.com/universities-embrace-artificial-intelligence-to-support-students/

Fourtané, S. (2021). *Artificial intelligence plays key role in the future of higher education.* Fierce Education. Retrieved from https://www.fierceeducation.com/best-practices/artificial-intelligence-critical-to-future-higher-education-0

Gardner, L. (2018). How A. I. is infiltrating every corner of the campus. *Chronicle of Higher Education, 64*(31), 11. Retrieved from https://www.chronicle.com/article/How-AI-Is-Infiltrating-Every/243022

Global Market Insights. (2022). AI in education market size &; share, growth forecast 2022–2030. Retrieved from https://www.gminsights.com/industry-analysis/artificial-intelligence-ai-in-education market#:~:text=Artificial%20Intelligence%20%28AI%29%20in%20Education%20Market%20size%20exceeded,experience%20is%20likely%20to%20drive%20the%20industry%20growth

Wiley University Contributors. (2022). 5 ways artificial intelligence may influence higher education. Wiley University Series. Retrieved from https://universityservices.wiley.com/artificial-intelligence-in-higher-ed-admissions-retention/

Zeide, E. (2019). *Artificial intelligence in higher education: Applications, promise and perils, and ethical questions.* EDUCAUSE Review. Retrieved from https://er.educause.edu/articles/2019/8/artificial-intelligence-in-higher-education-applications-promise-and-perils-and-ethical-questions

Zharovskikh, A. (2020). *How face recognition and AI are used in healthcare.* InData Labs. Retrieved from https://indatalabs.com/blog/ai-face-recognition-in-healthcare

Chapter 5

Artificial Intelligence
and Agriculture

Jeffery Parsons

The field of agriculture is of critical importance to society, the economy, and even national security. It is no surprise then that agriculture has been an important focus of land grant universities, community colleges, and research institutes around the nation and the world. North Carolina alone has 19 community colleges that are approved to offer Agribusiness Technology programs and six that are approved to offer Applied Animal Science Technology (North Carolina Community College System, 2022).

Given the projected growth in world population and the growing demand for agricultural products, technology is expected to play an important role in meeting the needs of the future. Artificial intelligence (AI) and deep machine learning are among the new technologies that will alter the face of agriculture and agricultural education in the coming decades. A recent review of AI in agriculture by Subhalaxmi stated, "The new agricultural systems must be more productive in terms of production, more efficient in terms of operation, more resilient to global climate change, and far more sustainable for future generations" (2021, p. 41).

Farmers need to be able to produce more output while utilizing fewer resources like pesticides, fertilizers, and water. Accomplishing this will require connecting numerous technologies and processing large amounts of data to make decisions and carry out related tasks. AI ". . . is a synthetic intelligence function that mimics the human brain . . . [and] can be utilized in decision-making" (Subhalaxmi, 2021, p. 41).

The growing role of technology and AI in agriculture will naturally alter higher education agriculture programs. Indeed, those changes are already happening. This chapter will explore the impact of AI on agriculture and higher education today. It will also look ahead and predict how AI will change agricultural education by 2032 and 2050.

ARTIFICIAL INTELLIGENCE IN AGRICULTURAL EDUCATION TODAY

AI is already impacting the field of agriculture as evidenced by the application of IBM's Environmental Intelligence Suite to regenerative agriculture. According to a publication from IBM's The Weather Company, "the platform works with your existing IT, cloud and software-as-a-service (SaaS) infrastructure to create a security-rich digital replica of your farm and an electronic field record that is accessible for all authorized uses" (CIO Insights, 2019, p. 6).

Combining weather forecasts and data such as soil moisture and pH, drone-provided imagery, workflow data, and genetic information about plants, IBM's Watson-powered system helps farmers make decisions about planting, irrigation, harvesting, and other critical agricultural tasks. One customer, E & J Gallo Winery, credits IBM's AI system with a 26% increase in yields along with "improved grape quality" and "reduced water usage" (CIO Insights, 2019, p. 9).

Another example of AI already in use is the 2019 New Holland combine. The combine's "Field and Yield Prediction System is a self-learning tool that predicts changes in slope and crop density in front of the combine" (Sheldon, 2018, p. 1). The machine can optimize its own settings by using GPS and topography data and measurements from "adjacent passes already harvested" (Sheldon, 2018, p. 1). Similar technologies are coming available on other pieces of large farm equipment.

Agriculture has a long history and many farmers are still using traditional methods. However, "96 percent of farms with sales of $1 million or more [are] reporting significant technology use" (Binkley, 2019, p. 1). According to the 2016 agriculture census, while nearly 50% of older farmers are utilizing technology, "70 percent or more of farmers in the age groups between 25 and 59 reported using technology in their operations" (Binkley, 2019, p. 1). The trend is for agriculture to become more technologically advanced and connected as the baton is passed to the upcoming generation.

The growing role of AI is already having an impact on higher education institutions with agriculture programs. North Carolina State University (NCSU) launched its AI Academy in 2020, to prepare students for careers in AI in a variety of fields, including both agriculture and education. Within the field of agriculture, the Academy is predicting that AI will be used for monitoring smart crops, predicting harvest rates, and operating agricultural robots.

Within the field of education, AI is predicted to be used for adaptive learning and virtual instructional opportunities (NC State University, 2022).

AI within agriculture is of significant research interest for many universities, internationally. For example, the engineering faculty at the University of Sydney in Australia are conducting research on how AI and automated systems can be used to improve outcomes for farmers. Vision systems with machine learning are being developed to monitor livestock appearances to determine the animal's well-being. Robots and unmanned aerial vehicles are being used to monitor farms and provide data to AI systems that can make decisions about planting, harvesting, irrigation, and livestock management.

Automated robotic systems are under development to help small farmers overcome workforce shortages and perform tasks like weeding and harvesting (The University of Sydney, n.d.). Companies like Microsoft are developing software and machine learning systems to take advantage of the data that can be gathered from modern farms. Additionally, Microsoft has created an educational version of its commercial FarmBeats technology to be used in secondary and post-secondary educational institutions.

The FarmBeats for Students program "combines an affordable hardware kit with curriculum and activities designed to give students hands-on experience in applying precision agriculture techniques to food production. Using an array of sensors, students stream and analyze data in Excel" (Microsoft, 2022). In addition to being given access to big data sets, students learn to build and train machine learning systems. "The program ends by introducing a responsible AI framework, engaging students with some of the social and ethical challenges raised by this new technology" (Microsoft, 2022).

High schools, community colleges, and universities with agriculture programs can make use of this type of resource in preparing students for new agricultural careers. Autonomous tractors are already in use on many larger farms as are automated robots that perform "complete cycles of agricultural work such as planting, spraying, and harvesting" (Ruiz-Real et al., 2020). This is requiring a new type of training for agriculture students who must understand the GIS mapping and GPS location systems utilized by autonomous vehicles. Even farm equipment and vehicle maintenance have changed.

Live data transfer from smart equipment can be transmitted to dealerships, allowing them to compile and analyze "machine data to make decisions regarding preventive maintenance and service. This gives dealerships and [Original Equipment Manufacturers] OEMs the ability to ensure their support department has the correct resources on hand and could potentially allow them to address the issue before it occurs" (Sheldon, 2018, p. 3). This has implications not only for how agriculture students are trained but ahow heavy equipment technicians need to be trained.

Unmanned Aerial Vehicles

Unmanned aerial vehicles (UAVs), also known as drones, have gained widespread usage in agriculture and are being incorporated into agriculture education programs. UAVs equipped with specialized sensors and cameras can be used to detect weeds, measure moisture levels in crop fields, and "detect and count citrus trees, estimate tree height and canopy size, and measure plant nutrient levels" (Giles, 2021, p. 21). A new cloud-based technology called AgroView has been developed that "uses AI algorithms to process, analyze, and visualize data being collected from aerial- and ground-based platforms" (Giles, 2021, p. 21).

The amount of data being gathered is staggering and goes beyond what humans can efficiently process without assistance. Making full use of the data available so that the most effective decisions can be made now requires the use of some type of AI system. Drones can also be used to manage livestock herds, "monitoring [for] illnesses, injuries, and even pregnancies" (Ben Ayed & Hanana, 2021, p. 4).

While drones were initially used for remote monitoring of livestock locations, the data from drones can now be combined with other "electro-optical, acoustical, mechanical, and biosensors" to determine the health and well-being of individual animals in the herd (Nayeri et al., 2019, p. 31). The data can be analyzed by an AI system in almost real-time to make decisions that benefit both the animal and the farmer. Farmers and agriculture faculty at colleges and universities are both currently dealing with an industry in flux.

AI, sensors, drones, robots, and autonomous vehicles are changing the industry in a way that has never been seen before. However, according to Talaviya et al.,

> handling realistic challenges faced by farmers and using autonomous decision-making solutions to solve them, farming is still at a nascent stage. In order to explore the scope of AI in agriculture . . . applications need to be more robust. (2020, p. 69)

In other words, more changes are coming to the field of agriculture and agriculture education. Educators must stay abreast of research be ready to adjust their curricula and training as needed.

ARTIFICIAL INTELLIGENCE IN
AGRICULTURAL EDUCATION BY 2032

By the year 2032, many of the technologies that are just being introduced in 2022 will be commonplace and enjoy widespread adoption across the agricultural industry. Other advancements that are still in the research phase may quickly enter the agricultural ecosystem. Higher education institutions will need to be ready to adapt and incorporate these new technologies into their training programs. This portion of the chapter will explore several technologies that could affect agricultural education by 2032.

Image Processing

Ireri et al. discuss the importance of vegetable sorting if growers are going to meet market standards and their product is to be easily packaged, sorted, and sold. Tomatoes, for example, must be inspected for "mechanical damage, disease, and insect damage, cracks, and pre-harvest deformation defects" (2019, p. 28). They must also be sorted by shape, size, and color. Machine learning technology combined with color image processing can be used to sort harvested tomatoes (or other produce) by several different features.

Another study by Rohani et al. uses similar technology to separate and recognize "the alive and dead eggs of rainbow trout" in a fish hatchery (2019, p. 27). Other groups of researchers are using machine learning "algorithms to predict the fruit ripening stages and fruit maturity" of strawberries and other fruits with amazing accuracy (Ben Ayed & Hanana, 2021, p. 3). The use of imaging technology and AI is not limited to static items like vegetables or fish eggs. It can also be used to recognize features of live animals.

An agricultural technology company headquartered in Ireland called Cainthus "provides a machine vision approach to create facial/pattern/objective recognition systems which are able to identify/classify individual cows/horse/sheep by their facial/body features in a few seconds, and enable considerable herds to be monitored with minimal human involvement" (Chen & Li, 2019, p. 119706). It can even detect signs of lameness or illness by cross-checking the animal's image with other pieces of data. Likely, this sort of advanced imaging technology in combination with AI and large data sets are commonplace on farms by 2032.

Impact on Education

Educational programs at community colleges and universities include courses and lab activities related to the use of imaging technology. Students need to

understand the setup and function of the equipment and know how to perform basic troubleshooting skills. Given the amount of money at stake in the
equipment and in the crop and/or livestock investments, it will be critically
important for students to know the capabilities and limitations of this technology. They will need to know how environmental factors could affect the
images and whether or not certain reference data sets used by the AI system
are more reliable than others.

Advanced imaging technology coupled with AI has the potential to identify
problems on a farm that could have previously gone unnoticed until it was too
late. Students should be taught not only how to use AI to identify problems
but also how to create quick solutions to those problems.

Weed Control

Weeds are a constant source of trouble for crop farmers and they are often
controlled by spraying entire fields with herbicides before planting and later
while crops are growing. Over-spraying of fields can result in financial
losses and environmental issues. Additionally, "the continued emergence of
herbicide-resistant weeds and the increasing labor costs are threatening the
ability of growers to manage weeds and maintain profits" (Su, 2020, p. 262).
The development of a smart farm system using imaging from tractors and
drones coupled with AI could be used to detect the location of weeds within
a field and distinguish weeds from crops.

This location data could be fed to herbicide sprayers on tractors that spray
only those areas of the field with the weeds. According to Giles, John Deere
is currently "working to commercialize a weed sprayer from Blue River
Technology that detects weeds and applies herbicides only to the weed"
(2021, p. 21). It is within the realm of possibility that imaging technology
coupled with machine learning could not only determine the location of
weeds in a field but also identify the species of individual weeds and then
recommend specific herbicides for specific weeds.

It is also possible that specially equipped drones carrying imaging technology and herbicide sprayers could be used instead of tractors with larger
sprayers. This would not only minimize the damage to the crops caused by
the larger equipment but also allow a greater degree of precision with the herbicide application. Agricultural education programs need to update their plant
science classes to note the increasing resistance of weeds to specific types of
herbicides. They will also need to include training on the imaging systems
and herbicide delivery options available to farmers at that time.

A variety of weed control options will likely be available to farmers in
2032. Therefore, the ability of students to conduct a cost-benefit analysis and

determine their return on investment will be critical to helping them choose the best option for their farm.

New Job Categories

Agricultural education programs in 2032 needed to adjust their programs to prepare students for careers and job titles that did not exist ten years earlier. Binkley (2019), writes that "in the not-too-distant future, farms will depend on hi-tech workers with titles like Tech-gronomist, Ag Tech Integrator and Knowledge Translators" (p. 1). The Tech-gronomist will recommend specific actions to farmers based on the evaluation of large data sets by AI systems. This person will perform the agricultural equivalent of a financial advisor, using large amounts of data and AI-based recommendations to make specific recommendations to farms in specific situations.

The Ag Tech Integrator will investigate technologies in use in other industries and then find ways to redesign them for use within the agricultural field. Knowledge Translators will focus on the development of brand-new technology for agriculture based on developing needs and new research discoveries (Binkley, 2019). These skill sets will not be seen as optional or extra but will be considered essential. Colleges and universities developed entirely new training programs within their agriculture departments. Additionally, these new programs are hybrid programs that share commonalities with engineering, information technology, and agriculture.

Business Operations

Agricultural businesses need to consider options, risks, profit margins, and economic forecasts. AI plays a large role in that aspect of farming by 2032. In the past, many farmers make their decisions based on experience with past results and consultation with other nearby farmers or with specialists who work with agricultural companies. By 2032, farmers are making use of information from AI systems using huge data sets to make their decisions about operational practices. Software can help farmers decide about things like seeding rates and expected yields. AI systems will support farming on a variety of fronts.

For example, AI takes "lists of transparent input prices, interest rates of various operating loans, 10 years of historic yield data and December corn futures to lay out various scenarios and make recommendations accordingly" (Sheldon, 2018, p. 4). For the retail end of the supply chain, AI is used "for predicting consumer demand, perception, and buying behavior" while also taking inventory management into account (Ben Ayed & Hanana, 2021, p.

4). The packaging and distribution phases of agricultural products are also affected by AI, becoming more efficient and less expensive.

The application of the Internet of Things (IoT) on farms combined with radio frequency identification and machine learning brought product tracing to a level that has not been seen before in agriculture. For example, the large-scale tracking of agricultural products over their complete life cycle has huge commercial benefits. It is particularly beneficial to "forming trust between the seller and buyer—by seeing the entire history of the product, the agricultural companies can make better decisions, find business partners wisely, and save time and money" (Zha, 2020, p. 3).

In 2032, AI systems are used to predict which new agricultural businesses or ventures will be successful and which ones will not (Horak, 2019, p. 2). Large-and small-scale farmers make use of these predictive systems before deciding to change their primary crops or livestock or before venturing into the agri-tourism industry. Agribusiness programs incorporate these decision-making tools into their coursework, teaching students how to make use of AI-generated recommendations while also understanding the limits of those recommendations.

While AI makes use of more and larger data sets than humans can, their recommendations are only as good as the validity of the data sets being used. Students need to understand this. They need to have a general sense of how economic systems work and how decisions have traditionally been made rather than becoming fully reliant on recommendations from AI systems. Thanks to the implementation of quantum computing, AI systems are no longer susceptible to being hacked by those with malintent.

Smart Farms and Plant Factories

The prevalence of smart farms or cyber-agriculture in 2032 has required agriculture programs in higher education to incorporate the use of sensors and information technology concepts within their programs.

They can monitor moisture levels in plants and, in indoor growing facilities, adjust the lighting to maximize the plant's health and output. While greenhouses have been used to accomplish this to some degree for centuries, the idea of a plant factory significantly increases the amount of control over the plants' environment. The plant factory artificially controls the "light, temperature, and water, to improve the production of crops, and also produce crops regardless of season and space, just as a factory produces products" (Hyunjin, 2020, p. 4).

Japanese and Korean companies have invested heavily in this sort of plant factory to not only shorten the growing period but to also grow produce in or near the cities where large parts of the population live. Such indoor growing technology is commonplace around the world since it minimizes the amount of transportation required between the producer and the end-user, lowering costs and minimizing greenhouse gas emissions. Smart farms operating outdoors could be tied into AI-predicted weather forecasts and adjust planting, irrigation, and harvesting schedules accordingly.

Imaging technology is used to detect various plant diseases and robots assist with harvesting tasks. Drones are used to monitor field conditions, report on moisture levels, and initiate targeted irrigation or fertilizing of those areas that need it (Jha et al., 2019, p. 10). AI technology like that on John Deere's AutoTrac system is commonplace in 2032. The system allows large pieces of farm equipment "to plant crops in a far more uniform and accurate way and can reduce overlap in agricultural processes such as tilling, planting and fertilizing, which in turn reduces the use of chemicals and increases productivity" (Chen & Li, 2019, p. 119706).

Other smart farm technologies that are commonplace in 2032 include "low-cost electronic noses and near-infrared spectroscopy" for the detection of pest infestations on crops (Fuentes & Tongson, 2021, p. 2). These sensors are used to detect scents emitted by an "aphid infestation in wheat plants and estimate plant physiological parameters using machine learning technology" (Fuentes & Tongson, 2021, p. 2). Tests have shown this technology to be highly accurate at predicting both the number of insects and determining the effects the infestation was having on the plants.

Drones are used to increase the level of monitoring the system can accomplish. These same drones could also become a potential delivery system for targeted pesticides. Other smart farm features monitor environmental conditions for livestock while on the farm and while being transported. The combination of sensors, data sets, and AI make it possible to predict milk productivity based on those environmental conditions and then work to alter those conditions to maximize animal welfare and production output.

According to Fuentes and Tongson (2021), this system "can be implemented in robotic and conventional dairy farms to respond more efficiently to climatic anomalies, such as cold stress or heat waves, to maintain animal welfare" (p. 2). Sensors are also used to "monitor the heart rate, respiration rate, and skin temperature of animals" to ensure the animal's welfare and preserve the farmer's capital investment during high-stress times such as transportation or heat waves (Fuentes and Tongson, 2021, p. 2).

To fully prepare students for the agriculture workforce in 2032, educational institutions find ways to expose students to working models of a smart farm and/or plant factory. This is accomplished by building small smart farms or plant factories on campus for students to use as a lab, much like many allied health programs have simulation hospitals for healthcare students to train in before attending clinicals. For colleges that do not have the budget to build a working smart farm on campus, partnerships are built with local smart farms.

The partnerships could consist of a memorandum of understanding that permits the college's agricultural program to use the partner's smart farm as a remote learning lab for its students, perhaps in return for students performing projects that benefit the smart farm. Another method is the development of internship and apprenticeship opportunities with smart farms or plant factories that allow students to take the theoretical knowledge learned in the classroom and apply it in a real production environment.

This provides the benefit of giving students work experience for their resumes and connecting them to an industry partner while allowing the college to avoid the expense of building a full smart farm. Instead, smaller trainers are utilized to help teach the concepts before students begin their internship or apprenticeship, which have the added benefit of providing the program faculty with real-time feedback from the industry about their training program. Weaknesses can be pointed out and corrected quickly and strengths can be reinforced.

ARTIFICIAL INTELLIGENCE IN AGRICULTURAL EDUCATION IN 2050

By the middle of the 21st century, AI plays a large role in many of the changes. As in 2032, higher education institutions adapted their agriculture programs in 2050 to meet the new training demands of the industry. To get an idea of the scope of the changes related to AI and agriculture in 2050, it is helpful to look at the most cutting-edge research that is currently happening. In March 2022, the University of Auburn hosted a conference that was funded by the USDA and was described as a joint effort of land grant universities in the United States.

The conference was titled, Envisioning 2050 in the Southeast: AI-Driven Innovations in Agriculture. Topics discussed at the conference included weather, agricultural automation, geospatial technologies like GIS and GPS, crop management, food processing, climate change, cloud computing, pest management, livestock monitoring and breeding, privacy, and university-industry partnerships (Auburn University, 2022). Auburn University described the purpose of the conference in this way:

Artificial intelligence (AI)-enabled decision support systems, automation and robotics have the potential to transform agriculture in the Southeast. Current challenges of growing population, climate change, water supply demands, shortage of labor, emerging pests and diseases, producing more with less, and customer demand for sustainable products place stress on the future of Southeastern agriculture.

However, incorporating AI into agriculture and food systems in the region can improve the productivity, efficiency and sustainability of agricultural practices and post-harvest processing, strengthen animal and crop breeding, reduce risks from pests and diseases, increase the quality and safety of food, strengthen farmers' advisory systems, and improve the resilience of agriculture in light of climate change. (Auburn University, 2022)

Back in 2022, the conference hosts and presenters expected AI to affect nearly every aspect of the agriculture industry from planning and production to distribution and retail by the middle of the 21st century. Partnerships between agricultural education programs and the agriculture industry will be paramount in 2050. Fast-changing technology will require research partnerships between industry and major universities. It will also require the nimble workforce training programs of community colleges.

Advanced Vision Systems and AI Processing

AI-enabled advanced vision systems were mentioned as a technology that agricultural education providers would need to adapt to by 2032 for crop and livestock monitoring and weed detection. In 2050, advancements in AI could make even more precise uses possible. For example, once crops grow to a certain size, detecting weeds with normal vision systems becomes more difficult because of the overlap of the crop plant and weeds. In 2050, however, genetic modifications to crop plants were designed so that particular crops exhibit particular fluorescent signals.

This "crop plant signaling is a new robot-plant interaction technique that allows the visualization of exogenous fluorescent signals applied to crop plants for crop/weed identification" (Su, 2020, p. 262). This technology is wide spread in 2050 across all types of crops, allowing AI-equipped drones with special sensors to discriminate between weeds and plants at any stage of crop plant growth and apply targeted amounts of herbicide to the detected weeds. The benefits to the farmer are cost and time savings and the benefits to the environment are fewer chemicals entering the soil and water table.

Other advancements in the AI processing of images provide more precise information to farmers that will help them better predict harvest times and expected yields. Talaviya et al. describe a burgeoning technology that will be commonplace by 2050 that does just that.

A robotic lens zooms in on the yellow flower of a tomato seedling. Images of the plant flow into an artificial intelligence algorithm that predicts precisely how long it will take for the blossom to become a ripe tomato ready for picking, packing, and the produce section of a grocery store. . . . (2020, p. 70)

Technologies like this and other AI-enabled advancements help increase global food production in 2050. In 2020, the United Nations predicted a 50% increase in production will be needed to feed an expected global population increase of 2 billion people. AI-enabled technology is critical to accomplishing this goal in conjunction with other new technologies. Environmental concerns limit previous strategies of simply plowing more land, diverting more water, or applying more pesticides and fertilizers (Talaviya et al. 2020). Higher education agricultural programs train students in the usage of new imaging and AI technologies.

Autonomous Pollination

Another field of agriculture in 2050 is autonomous pollination. Pollination, "which is a transfer of pollen from the anther (the flower's male organ) to the stigma (the female part of the flower)," is a critical part of the agricultural system. While some plants can self-pollinate, most are dependent on the pollen being transferred from one plant to another by the wind or pollinators like bees, butterflies, moths, and some birds. These living pollinators are so important to agriculture that Chen and Li (2019), report that "one-third of all food consumed by humans is the result of pollinators" (p. 119707).

However, pollinators have been in decline and are susceptible to pesticides, putting agricultural production at risk. One AI-based solution consists of "robotic micro air vehicle (MAV) pollinator[s]." These tiny, winged, robotic machines are controlled as a "robotic swarm" by an AI system capable of "complex problem-solving" (Chen & Li, 2019, p. 119707). The AI control system utilizes wireless signals to monitor the MAV swarm. In the 2020s, almond orchards in California and other crop growers around the country frequently rented honey bee hives that were driven on flat-bed trucks across the country to provide this pollination service.

This MAV technology has resulted in a whole new service industry needing trained technicians to support the pollination efforts of farms around the county by 2050. Community colleges and universities offer programs to train these technicians in MAV programming, repair, and operation.

Hybrids and Genetic Engineering

Hybridization has long been a technique used by farmers to develop stronger, hardier plants and livestock or to emphasize certain desirable features. Genetic engineering of plants and animals has taken this further by purposely editing the genome to try and create certain characteristics. However, there is still a lot of guesswork in determining which plants or animals to cross or which combination of genes to edit. Nayeri et al. (2019) report that machine learning is already being used to predict the outcome of animal breeding for certain characteristics. In 2050, AI systems altered plant and livestock breeding with genetic engineering.

Equipped with access to huge data sets of genetic information, machine learning algorithms, and massive processing power, AI systems suggest new hybrids or new genetic modifications to achieve the desired outcomes. In the same way that AI systems reinvented strategies for defeating chess masters, AI changes the way that livestock breeders and genetic engineers operate (Kissinger et al., 2021). Universities provide research and training programs related to this technology and the ethics and risks of its use. Community colleges ensure that their agriculture students know how to make use of breeding recommendations produced by AI.

Educational Simulators

Some AI systems are developed specifically for use by college agricultural programs. These AI-enabled software systems could simulate a multitude of different size crop and livestock operations located in any conceivable climate zone. With access to huge sets of weather and economic data, genomic information, and equipment maintenance and reliability data, these simulators could present students with particular scenarios. The student needs to choose the best course of action based on the given scenario.

Using machine learning, huge data sets, and processing power, these simulators predict the results that would likely occur based on the student's decision. More complicated scenarios could walk a student through the major decisions needing to be made over an entire year but compress the time to within an hour or two. Students could be asked to choose seeds, fertilizers, pesticides, planting and harvesting schedules, maintenance schedules, and even agricultural business partners and the system would provide feedback on the outcome of those choices. The benefits of such a system to students and faculty are obvious.

Ethical Issues

Much of this chapter has focused on the positive results of AI and machine learning in agriculture. However, there are some ethical issues that students in 2050 need to be aware of if they are going to use the technology appropriately. Colleges, researchers, businesses, and farmers need to keep these issues in mind and work to find solutions to them if AI is going to be beneficial to all of society and all farmers. Colleges need to find a way to help students in 2050 protect themselves and others from the potential unintended outcomes of AI.

The first ethical challenge is unemployment. Ben Ayed and Hanana (2021), point out that "smart machines and robots could replace the majority of the repetitive work and tasks" in the agriculture industry (p. 4). This could cause a huge loss of employment for many low-wage, undereducated farm workers like migrant workers that make up much of the agricultural workforce today. Colleges will need to work with government and industry partners to find ways to reach those who are displaced by AI technology and help them retrain for jobs in the new economy.

A second ethical challenge is the sheer cost of the advanced technology that will be needed for farms to remain competitive. The cost of upfitting a farm with smart farm technology and then maintaining the physical equipment, updating the software, and paying subscription fees to data sets and AI resources could be prohibitive for small farms (Ben Ayed & Hanana, 2021). Colleges need to incorporate training specific to smaller, local farm operations to help them identify niche markets where they can succeed. They will also need training on how to choose which technologies will be beneficial to their profitability and which ones are not.

Finally, there are ethical issues related to the power held by technology providers over farmers in 2050. Colleges need to make sure their students are aware of these issues and know how to identify abuses in the system. Ryan, M. (2019) points out that Agricultural Big Data Analytics could "be used as a form of manipulative power to initiate cheap land grabs and acquisitions . . . by pressuring farmers into situations they would not have otherwise chosen (such as installing monitors around their farm [or limiting] access to their farm and machinery)" (p. 49).

CONCLUSION

AI and other smart technologies are already changing the world of agriculture and agriculture education. This chapter has presented how AI technology could continue to alter agriculture and education programs over the next 10 years and also into the mid-21st century. AI has the potential to increase profits, minimize negative environmental impacts, and increase production to feed a growing world population. However, there are potential ethical issues that could arise. Colleges and universities will need to constantly adjust to industry needs while also remaining aware of issues that could negatively impact their students and community.

CHAPTER SUMMARIES

- Given the projected growth in world population and the growing demand for agricultural products, technology is expected to play an important role in meeting the needs of the future.
- The growing role of technology and AI in agriculture will naturally alter higher education agriculture programs.
- AI, sensors, drones, robots, and autonomous vehicles are changing the industry in a way that has never been seen before.
- The FarmBeats for Students program "combines an affordable hardware kit with curriculum and activities designed to give students hands-on experience in applying precision agriculture techniques to food production" (MicroSoft, 2022).
- Advanced imaging technology coupled with AI has the potential to identify problems on a farm that could have previously gone unnoticed until it was too late.
- It is also possible that specially equipped drones carrying imaging technology and herbicide sprayers could be used instead of tractors with larger sprayers.
- While AI makes use of more and larger data sets than humans can, their recommendations are only as good as the validity of the data sets being used.
- AI technology like that on John Deere's AutoTrac system is commonplace in 2032.
- Partnerships between agricultural education programs and the agriculture industry will be paramount in 2050.
- One AI-based solution consists of "robotic micro air vehicle (MAV) pollinator[s]."
- Some AI systems are developed specifically for use by college agricultural programs.
- However, there are some ethical issues that students in 2050 need to be aware of if they are going to use the technology appropriately.
- AI has the potential to increase profits, minimize negative environmental impacts, and increase production to feed a growing world population.

REFERENCES

Auburn University: Alabama Agriculture Experiment Station. (2022). *Envisioning 2050 in the Southeast: AI-driven innovations in agriculture.* https://aaes.auburn.edu/ai-driven-innovations-in-agriculture/

Ben Ayed, R., & Hanana, M. (2021). Artificial intelligence to improve the food and agriculture sector. *Journal of Food Quality, 2021,* 1–7.

Binkley, A. (2019). Future farm workers will need a new set of skills; as larger farms adapt new technology, future workers will need hi-tech skills. *Ontario Farmer,* B.10.

Chen, Y., & Li, Y. (2019). Intelligent autonomous pollination for future farming: A micro air vehicle conceptual framework with artificial intelligence and human-in-the-loop. *IEEE Access, 7,* 119706–119707.

The Weather Company: An IBM Business. (2019). *CIO Insights: The future of intelligent farming and food supply chain management.*

Fuentes, S., & Tongson, E. J. (2021). Implementation of sensors and artificial intelligence for environmental hazards assessment in urban, agriculture and forestry systems. *Sensors* (Basel, Switzerland), *21*(19), 6383.

Giles, F. (2021). How artificial intelligence will drive the future of agriculture. *Western Fruit Grower, 141*(3), 20–21.

Horák, J. (2019). Using artificial intelligence to analyse businesses in agriculture industry. *SHS Web of Conferences, 61,* 1005.

Hyunjin, C. (2020). A study on the change of farm using artificial intelligence focused on smart farms in Korea. *Journal of Physics.* Conference Series, *1642*(1), 12025.

Ireri, D., Belal, E., Okinda, C., Makange, N., & Ji, C. (2019). A computer vision system for defect discrimination and grading in tomatoes using machine learning and image processing. *Artificial Intelligence in Agriculture, 2,* 28–37.

Jha, K., Doshi, A., Patel, P., & Shah, M. (2019). A comprehensive review on automation in agriculture using artificial intelligence. *Artificial Intelligence in Agriculture, 2,* 1–12.

Kissinger, H. A., Schmidt, E., & Huttenlocher, D. (2021). *The age of AI and our human future.* Little, Brown, and Company.

Microsoft. (2022, April 8). *FarmBeats for students.* https://docs.microsoft.com/en-us/learn/educator-center/instructor-materials/farmbeats-for-students

Nayeri, S., Sargolzaei, M., & Tulpan, D. (2019). A review of traditional and machine learning methods applied to animal breeding. *Animal Health Research Reviews, 20*(1), 31–46.

North Carolina Community College System. (2022, May 23). *North Carolina Community College System Catalog.* https://www.nccommunitycolleges.edu/academic-programs/nc-community-college-system-catalog

NC State University. (2022). *Join the Artificial Intelligence Academy.* The AI Academy. https://ai-academy.ncsu.edu/

Rohani, A., Taki, M., & Bahrami, G. (2019). Application of artificial intelligence for separation of live and dead rainbow trout fish eggs. *Artificial Intelligence in Agriculture, 1,* 27–34.

Ruiz-Real, J. L., Uribe-Toril, J., Arriaza, J., & Valenciano, J. (2020). A look at the past, present and future research trends of artificial intelligence in agriculture. *Agronomy* (Basel), *10*(11), 1839.

Ryan, M. (2019; 2020). Agricultural big data analytics and the ethics of power. *Journal of Agricultural & Environmental Ethics, 33*(1), 49–69.

Sheldon, B. (2018, October 17). Where artificial intelligence could take agriculture. *Farm Industry News*.

Su, W. (2020). Crop plant signaling for real-time plant identification in smart farm: A systematic review and new concept in artificial intelligence for automated weed control. *Artificial Intelligence in Agriculture*, *4*, 262–271.

Subhalaxmi. (2021). Smart agriculture using artificial intelligence: A review. *I-Manager's Journal on Computer Science*, *9*(2), 41.

Talaviya, T., Shah, D., Patel, N., Yagnik, H., & Shah, M. (2020). Implementation of artificial intelligence in agriculture for optimisation of irrigation and application of pesticides and herbicides. *Artificial Intelligence in Agriculture*, *4*, 58–73.

The University of Sydney. (n.d.). *Agriculture and the environment*. https://www.sydney.edu.au/engineering/our-research/robotics-and-intelligent-systems/australian-centre-for-field-robotics/agriculture-and-the-environment.html

Zha, J. (2020). Artificial intelligence in agriculture. *Journal of Physics*. Conference Series, *1693*(1), 12058.

Chapter 6

Artificial Intelligence and Healthcare

Jannylle Pitter

Healthcare is continuously evolving in order to provide patients with the best care. Technology, including artificial intelligence (AI), assists in advancing healthcare services for practitioners and clients. AI uses machine intelligence for reasoning and decision-making instead of a living organism such as a human or animal (Rawat et al., 2022).

AI assists healthcare professionals accurately diagnose and treat medical conditions, improving recovery, and decreasing the length of stays in medical facilities. AI can quickly assess health records and patient symptoms to facilitate improved healthcare outcomes (Guo et al., 2020).

NATURAL LANGUAGE PROCESSING AND DOCUMENTATION

Natural Language Processing

AI has been instrumental in developing natural language processes (NLP) within healthcare. NLP is a category within AI that uses algorithms and models capable of assessing language. NLP is a technology that can recognize the linguistic context (Botelle et al., 2022). The combination of AI and NLP in healthcare is built upon using millions of networks that are structured data points to synthesize information (Baclic et al., 2020). It is used in electronic health records to extract information from electronic health records (EHR) (Ayre et al., 2021).

In healthcare, NLP has been developed to analyze and extract medical information related to diagnoses, symptoms, or treatments as documented in the medical records of a specific patient. The development of NLP has evolved over the last decade. Prior systems used matching systems and logic rules to search available data; however, these technologies yielded minimal usable results for healthcare workers. With the improvements in machine learning, additional features using broad access coverage and neural network algorithms were added to current NLP models (Botelle et al., 2022).

Electronic Health Record Systems

Healthcare workers are required to document all services and interactions that occur with the clients. EHR are digital charts that include a patient's medical information that can easily be accessed by providers that are part of a patient's care team (Ayre et al., 2021). AI related to EHR has shown success when predicting patient outcomes for individuals with sepsis and echocardiography (Bohr & Memarzadeh et al., 2020; Noorbakhsh-Sabet et al., 2019). Improvements to EHR can assist providers with completing treatments and providing medications using streamlined systems.

Healthcare providers can also quickly extract information keywords by searching all of the client's charts at once instead of using single search options previously used. The use of the cloud is also on the rise within healthcare services. Cloud computing involves collecting data using remote services and managing and storing patient healthcare records and information. The cloud allows for faster healthcare service delivery and improves the ability to access information without the limitations of a physical location (Pacis et al., 2018).

Application to Healthcare Programs Documentation

Healthcare programs provide students with opportunities to practice written clinical skills. When teaching skills, the process of accurate documentation, programs must intentionally include opportunities for students to utilize electronic documentation programs that include natural language processing when accessing EHR. Collaboration with clinical settings that use these types of technology can also be included in practicum experiences for additional opportunities to reinforce learning (Bohr & Memarzadeh et al., 2020).

DIAGNOSIS AND TREATMENT APPLICATIONS

Predictive Technology

In the medical field, technology and predictive models can provide clinicians with the tools to make accurate patient care decisions. Using predictive technology can improve medical data access and reduce medical costs. Predictive technology uses machine learning techniques by monitoring a system and relaying it to a human response. Once this information is stored, the response can be replicated when the same condition occurs in the future. Technology can decode and review large amounts of information quickly while monitoring patient data, which assists medical professionals with making decisions related to patient care (Battineni et al., 2020).

Genomic Medicine

Technology and its role within healthcare are continuously evolving. Nanotechnology is the research of biological objects at the molecular state. AI has increased alongside the development of research focused on atomic structures and how healthcare can be improved using this new form of technology (Rawat et al., 2022). Sequencing of a person's genetic information is a concept that is gaining popularity. Genomic medicine provides opportunities to enhance current capabilities to identify specific genes and mutations using AI to interpret a person's genome pattern and sequence (Quazi, 2022).

Genomic medicine can assist with technology that identifies facial features to aid in the early detection of genetic disorders. Genomic medicine also shows a solid process in oncology through the comparison of benign tissues with those mutated (National Human Research Institute, 2019). AI algorithms take information and identify similarities in patterns and genetic information. The diagnosis of diseases relies on genomic medicine identifying pathogenic variants compared to non-diseased genetic information. Specific mapping allows for high-level diagnostics that improve the speed of analyzing medical data (Dias & Torkamani, 2019).

Clustered Regularly Interspaced Short Palindromic Repeats (CRISPR)

The advancement of science in the healthcare sector is continually becoming more sophisticated to meet patients' needs. In 1990, technology was utilized to determine how DNA creates proteins and stores this information within a cell (Hunnicutt et al., 2018). A breakthrough in the Human Genome project occurred in 2003 when the entire DNA sequence of humans and other species was completed. Scientists are now able to replicate DNA in days versus years. As medical technology continues to develop and become more refined, a new system of DNA replication and modification in bacteria has been developed.

The new system of DNA replication that was discovered is called CRISPR (Clustered Regularity Interspaced Short Palindromic Repeats). CRISPR allows DNA strands to be modified with improved accuracy and in less time using technology (Hunnicutt et al., 2018). When CRISPR segments were analyzed, the researchers discovered that the cells could act protectively. The development of CRISPR allowed bacteria to recognize a virus previously infected with and store this information inside its DNA to create a defense response against the virus in the future (Hunnicutt et al., 2018).

Colorectal cancer is the second leading cause of cancer-related deaths in the United States and Western Countries (Datta et al., 2018). Researchers have discovered that 30% of colorectal cancers are genetic and can be inherited through risk alleles identified as single nucleotide polymorphisms (SNPs). The SNPs have a racial predictor and have been linked to higher rates of colorectal cancers in Black people compared to White people and other socio-economic disparities (Datta et al., 2018). Participants in a research study gave consent to have a biopsy sample from normal rectal mucous.

This sample was compared to the researchers' colorectal samples in a laboratory. CRISPR gene techniques were used to change the DNA of SNPs cells. The researchers were able to design the CRISPR cells to recreate the risk allele and alternate the mutation (Datta et al., 2018)

Triple-negative breast cancer (TNBC) is characterized by the loss of an estrogen receptor, progesterone receptor, and human growth factor. In 2019, of all the new breast cancers diagnosed, 12% were TNBC cases.

Women of African origin have a higher incidence rate of carrying the hereditary TNBC gene mutation. Currently, very few treatment interventions are available to treat TNBC; therefore, patients typically utilize surgeries, chemotherapy, and radiation as treatment options. To provide patients with other effective treatment therapies, researchers developed a tumor-targeting CRISPR genome to edit the mutation seen in the cells of TNBC. These CRISPR cells targeted DNA sequences to suppress tumor growth. This new technology represents a new delivery platform for treating women with breast cancer (Guo et al., 2019).

CRISPR research is an emerging practice area within the biological and medical fields. Secondary schools have already started to introduce technology surrounding CRISPR to students. Advancements within CRISPR are driving down the price of tools needed to perform these potential life-saving interventions.

Nanotechnology and Applications to Healthcare Programs

The development of nanotechnology is vital to continue healthcare advancements. Educational leaders must consider how changes in nanotechnology will impact students' roles in the workplace. Students need to understand what genetic-based technology exists to make appropriate referrals and educate clients about their medical conditions. Higher educational institution leaders will need to purchase tools that can be used to provide students with practical learning experiences (Hunnicutt et al., 2018).

Biotechnology programs in higher educational institutions have integrated components of CRISPR education into the current curriculum programs. Students learn skills in the areas that focus on cell culture, DNA manipulation, and interpreting biological data. Developing research-based programs in higher educational institutions is rooted in close interactions with biotechnology companies and administrators to ensure that the skills taught reflect what is needed to practice in the field.

APPS FOR HEALTH AND WELLNESS

Many supplements to healthcare are available using artificial intelligence and apps that can track the health and wellness of patients. AI has expanded medical services allowing for increased connectivity and analyzability remotely without the physical distance becoming a barrier (Mamdiwar et al., 2021).

Wearables and Health Tracking Apps

Technology that can be connected to individuals can assist with monitoring a person's health needs. The concept of using the internet to connect devices to allow them to monitor vital signs, activity level, and location are constantly evolving within the healthcare sector. Patients can be monitored throughout the day by healthcare providers. They can receive information critical to medication or therapy intervention changes to assist with treating a disease or medical condition and assist with cost-effectiveness when managing patient care (Mamdiwar et al., 2021).

Occupational therapy is a profession that involves the rehabilitation of clients across the lifespan using functional occupations as therapeutic modalities (Liu, 2018). As occupational therapists (OTs) enter the new technology era, it presents opportunities to enable clients in meaningful occupations. Technology encompasses many parts of a person's life, including places where people live, work environments, and items that can be worn daily (Lui,

2018). The Internet of Things (IoT) is an element of this era that is driving the future.

This type of technology is being used in smart eyewear developed by a manufacturer in Japan. Smart eyewear collects data about clients using sensors embedded in the frames of the glasses. OTs can use the data obtained to determine if clients who suffered from a stroke are using compensatory strategies to improve areas of inattention to their body's affected side. The client can use smart glasses while driving, walking, and performing everyday tasks. OTs can track the client's head, eye, and neck movements with the data received to provide feedback about their ability to use the compensatory strategies given during therapy sessions (Lui, 2018).

There are many uses for wearable technology. Currently, over 160,000 apps on Android and Apple devices provide access to health, diet, and exercise-based programs (Goodyear et al., 2018). Apps can be downloaded onto devices to track a person's fitness level throughout the day. Based on data the person loads about their height, weight, and body type, the devices use sensors to read a person's blood oxygen level, heart rate, and pulse to determine how many calories are expended during activities. Research has indicated that the data obtained from wearable devices is valid (Mamdiwar et al., 2021).

Telemedicine

Using digital technology to communicate and perform consultations, medical examinations, or interdisciplinary collaboration falls under the medical service of telemedicine. Telemedicine aims to reduce the gap in medical services by reducing costs and delays when providing patient care. AI is regularly used during telemedicine interventions. Through telemedicine, costs of tests and in-person appointments are reduced while the speed of medical services is increased. Patient monitoring systems include wireless sensors that measure a person's vitals and track the data to note progression or changes (Pacis et al., 2018).

Telerehabilitation

Delivering therapy through telerehabilitation is growing, especially for those that live in rural areas. Smartphones and tablets have led to the emergence of the Rehabilitation IoT in a person's home. A study was completed with 140 adult participants who suffered a stroke. The participants' functional performance was assessed using Rehabilitation IoT in their homes. The study participants were provided with ankle sensors inside their house daily while information was transmitted to a smartphone. Participants did not need to carry the phone during the day as the information from the sensors were transmitted wirelessly at night.

The information from the phone was sent to a central server for the therapists to analyze. The therapists learned about the patients' gait patterns using measurable data that analyzed speed, distance, and duration of activities completed. The patients received feedback from the therapists about strategies that could be implemented to decrease a sedentary lifestyle (Dobkin, 2017).

Health and Wellness Apps and the Application to Healthcare Programs

Students and faculty have access to health apps for personal use. Healthcare programs must integrate how items used for personal use can benefit healthcare professionals in the treatment and monitoring of diseases or illnesses. Learning the components of programming apps on different platforms is vital to educating patients about using technology in their natural environments. Students and clinicians must understand how to use this information to make clinical decisions. Higher education leaders follow up with product developers in order for students to learn on tools that are relevant to what is being used (Mamdiwar et al., 2021).

VIRTUAL, AUGMENTED REALITY AND BLOCKCHAIN TECHNOLOGY

Virtual and Augmented Reality

The rise of virtual and augmented reality can be seen in many sectors, including healthcare. Virtual reality (VR) and augmented reality (AR) have impacted how technology is used in healthcare settings and teaching applications. VR incorporates computers to create a simulated environment, which places the user inside the virtual realm. A head-mounted display is used while inside this simulated virtual world. A user can utilize their senses to interact with the environment. Virtual reality does have its limitations, as its capabilities are impacted directly by computer processing abilities (Patel & Gonsalves, 2022; Pottle, 2019).

VR provides the user with a unique experience as they can learn from the experiences within the virtual environment (Pottle, 2019). AR is a technology that allows virtual objects to be superimposed within current reality. AR uses virtual images that are computer generated and augments these images by placing them into the person's current environment, allowing for a blended interaction between the person and technology. When technology functions optimally, AR can seamlessly interact with the environment without any lags in connections (Patel & Gonsalves, 2022).

Blockchain Technology

A blockchain is a system used to generate and store data securely. The process includes a segment of the blockchain being removed when another transaction occurs, followed by another blockchain connection being made. The information on how the block is shared, changed, or accessed is stored on a secure network that can only be accessed by those connected to the original blockchain (Siyal et al., 2019). Blockchains are timed and stamped to quickly identify when changes were made and by which person or organization.

The healthcare sector has been a victim of hacking of patient information that needs to be protected, as stated in government-related policies. Blockchain technology operates using strong security standards and reliability. The interaction between multiple team members that have been given access to the blockchain allows various healthcare professionals to review and provide input about a patient without a location as a potential boundary.

Virtual, Augmented Reality and Blockchain Application in Healthcare Programs

VR can benefit healthcare educators, learners, and systems. The convenience of VR makes it a complementary addition to education in healthcare. With the use of a laptop and a head-mounted display, learners can engage within a virtual environment that is safe and easy to use. VR environments are repeatable and allow learners multiple opportunities to make mistakes and learn from them in a predictable environment. Since VR learning experiences can be controlled, it allows for standardized approaches to be implemented before implementing interventions on clients (Pottle, 2019).

Practicing complex skills in a simulated environment before interacting with human clients helps to improve critical thinking and decision-making skills for practitioners. With technology, students must become proficient in ensuring that medical and health-related data remains safe. Introducing students to new concepts they may experience in healthcare settings better prepares them to understand the benefits and risks of technology such as blockchain (Pottle, 2019).

ARTIFICIAL INTELLIGENCE AND
TECHNOLOGY IN HEALTHCARE IN 2032

Technology changes are noted throughout all sectors of the economy, including healthcare. AI has been used to enhance how practitioners can serve patients and allow patients to be informed consumers of healthcare products. Currently, there is a shift from providing care to patients at the acute level and shifting toward preventative care. Coupling this shift with AI helps to streamline healthcare services available to clients (Garson & Levin, 2021; Haick & Tang, 2021). The United States allocates more money on healthcare-related spending than any other country.

However, it ranks low on health rankings, including life expectancy, infant mortality, and quality of life. Changing the current healthcare model to a preventative and wellness model will allow the county to invest money in programs that reduce health disparities from occurring and save money and lives (Benjamin, 2011). Technology can help bridge this gap and access more significant amounts of patients to provide early intervention to medical conditions identified.

Predictive Technology

AI and predictive technology allow medical practitioners to understand better the changes that occur in patients with increased accuracy and details. The data that can be obtained through predictive technology provides insight into immediate medical concerns but can also track information related to dietary intake, environmental and work conditions, air, water quality, additional housing, and the safety of a person's physical environment. This information will allow healthcare practitioners to determine the risk factors of when a person may be at greater risk of becoming ill (Bohr & Memarzadeh, 2020).

Predictive technology also creates opportunities for the early detection of disease or illness by quickly reviewing client data to note changes in medical stats that can alter medical professionals to a potential problem before symptoms may occur (Noorbakhsh-Sabet et al., 2019). The location of healthcare services is also imperative to predictive technology. In the next ten years, a hospital will no longer be the only location where patients receive care. Patients can access care at community-based medical facilities, same-day medical clinics, specialized treatment facilities, or even at the patient's home.

These locations can all use technology to allow medical staff to monitor a patient's post-medical procedure in real time. The location of the patient of clinical is no longer the central component in healthcare delivery; technology that binds these individuals together is needed to connect vital data to support rehabilitation (Vatandsoost & Litkouhi, 2019). Reducing the need for transportation can increase client participation in follow-up healthcare as it reduces any barriers that patients may face for those that live in areas without public transportation or direct access to a vehicle, or the option to pay for transportation.

Wearables and Apps

The use of wearables and apps on mobile devices allows patients to have access to their healthcare information throughout the day. As wearable devices and apps evolve and have more sophisticated capabilities, new features will be added. Currently, devices offer wearables that can detect falls of an individual (Sabry et al., 2022). Eating apps are in development to monitor the dietary concerns of clients. Based on the data obtained from wearables, a medical professional can access the times of day a client eats and their impact on blood glucose levels. Drinking and smoking apps can also be used to track and monitor health-related behaviors (Sabry et al., 2022).

Stress and well-being are directly related to the mental health of individuals. Monitoring patients' heart rates and blood pressure can detect changes and stress on the body. The data that is used in wearables can notify clients who have seizures of the possible episode. This type of alert will allow the patient to take precautions to locate a safe area or ask for assistance in the possibility of a medical emergency (Sabry et al., 2022).

Healthcare Bots and Natural Language Processing

The implementation of interactive chat services or chatbots incorporates the use of NPL to answer patient questions or statements. Healthcare bots can be used to refill prescriptions, schedule appointments, or collect payments. Patients are provided better care when actively involved in their medical treatment plan. Using digital services to ask questions and get medical feedback improves the patient experience in healthcare settings. Healthcare bots also allow medical professionals to complete more involved tasks that allow them to work directly with patients or other medical practitioners (Powell, 2019).

Virtual and Augmented Reality

The application and use of VR in healthcare have directly impacted how medical services are delivered. VR allows students and clinicians to practice and train in simulated environments that are controlled and safer for errors to occur before being introduced to patients. VR can also be used post-surgery in rehabilitative or work-hardening programs for patients. It can simulate a therapeutic environment where a client can experience feelings of calm, reduced anxiety, and happiness. Placing clients in virtual environments allows the therapist to work better with the client outside of the virtual world (Patel & Gonsalves, 2022).

VR has a vital role in the areas of education and training of healthcare practitioners. This technology can be used for emergency training services to allow students to observe how experts in the field intervene in these scenarios. Students can also live stream into settings, observe how other professionals manage patients, and understand disease-specific interventions.

HEALTHCARE PROGRAMS IN 2032

Healthcare programs must change with the advancements in technology. By 2032, it is expected that the use of technology will be embedded within all student learning activities. Students may have some knowledge about technology-based applications from personal use; however, educators will bridge learning to emphasize the importance of technology for bettering patient care. Preventative treatment approaches are being utilized due to the reduction in health-related costs. Technology is a critical factor in preventive intervention and early detection and monitoring of potential diseases or illnesses (Garson & Levin, 2001; Wiens & Shenoy, 2017).

ARTIFICIAL INTELLIGENCE AND TECHNOLOGY IN HEALTHCARE IN 2050

Reduction of Physical Hospitals and Clinics

The Coronavirus Disease 19 (Covid-19) pandemic has brought about many changes in healthcare services and delivery. During the Covid-19 pandemic, there was a shift toward providing care to patients with significant medical complications in a hospital setting. Patients with fewer complex symptoms were often treated through alternative means such as community-based programs that utilized a drive-through approach or telemedicine services. This shift was implemented to reduce direct exposure of the virus to others and lower the number of symptomatic patients in a community.

A direct result of this shift is that more patients prefer to receive medical services in a personal space instead of the traditional clinic or hospital settings. Consumers of services strive to streamline access to medical services for increased convenience (Kumar et al., 2021). In the future, patients should expect a reduction in the number of physical medical buildings and only expect to enter these buildings if they have extreme symptoms. Utilizing other medical staff or robotics to complete home visits will also rise as medical facilities become less common (Kumar et al., 2021; Vatandsoost & Litkouhi, 2019).

Technology to Improve Productivity

Although AI can be seen as replacing workers in some economic sectors, healthcare professionals have embraced technology. AI and healthcare complement one another as medical professionals see the direct benefit of reduced workload, which heightens productivity. Tasks such as completing chart reviews, prescribing medications, and clinical documentation and billing can all be completed using AI. Speech recognition that is used within all documentation and billing platforms will significantly reduce the time spent charting patient records. Reducing repetitive tasks help improve morale and personnel well-being (Diaz and Torkamani, 2019).

Shift from Wearables to Implantable

AI can be seen in mobile devices that consumers use to monitor their health information. Most devices that track health data are either worn on the body or through a mobile device (Li et al., 2020). Technology implanted internally in the body will become more common in the future. Healthcare professionals benefit from the ability to monitor patients continually outside the hospital or clinic through wearable technology. Information such as changes in heart rate or blood glucose levels can automatically alert the patient that they may be experiencing a heart attack or diabetic emergency. Healthcare can be managed in real time.

Genomic Medicine and Reimbursement

As more research is completed in the field of genome development, its acceptance will change. As general knowledge about this AI form increases, negative perceptions will be reshaped. Genomic medicine can be used to prevent diseases and improve the quality of life for humans. Currently, assess to genomic medicine is not expected due to associated costs. Evidence to support its safety and reliability will highlight the importance of this type of medical intervention in providing patient care. As a result, insurance companies shift reimbursement policies, allowing more patients to benefit from the non-traditional medical services offered.

Blockchain for Payments and Medical Records

Medical records must comply with government regulations protecting a patient's personal and medical information. Over the years, storing information using cloud devices has made data breaches more common and puts data at risk. Blockchain technology can be used to safely transmit data and also make payments for medical services rendered. Patients will have increased autonomy over their medical and financial records through accessing blockchains to see when medical staff or insurance companies open medical records. Patients will remain in the chain of the sequence of events on the blockchain and can monitor for suspicious activity.

HEALTHCARE PROGRAMS IN 2050

Educational leaders will change educational standards and program delivery based on available technology. By 2050, many healthcare programs will be conducted using a hybrid teaching model, with options for clinical rotations using simulated experiences or virtual reality to display competencies. Students will have early access to interact with clients before entering a hospital or clinical setting using technology to simulate various conditions in their home learning environment or the classroom.

Training in technology will also occur earlier within the didactic curriculum to prepare students for the face pace healthcare environment and the use of digital documentation, patient visits, and monitoring of patient medical records. The use of technology to monitor patient data will be a large part of medical practitioners' role. Healthcare workers will no longer wait for clients to make appointments and review medical charts when concerns arise. Instead, there will be continuous routine monitoring of symptoms and medical information to allow for early intervention and limit the risk of disease progression (Thimblebly, 2013).

Students and faculty will also have the option to interact with robots as educators. As the new generation of learners enters higher education, they have a stronger connection to the use of the technology in their daily lives. Students feel more comfortable learning from technology and tend have a good understanding of how to use chatbots, email and virtual meetings to supplement face-to-face learning. The amount of time spent in the classroom will decrease, as virtual learning will allow students to be in control of identify the best environment to learn in their natural setting.

Payment of tuition will also change throughout educational programs. The use of cyber-funding and blockchains will help to increase student financial security and information related to privacy. The payments used in educational settings will be generalizable to healthcare establishments and can assist with bridging learning using different payment platforms.

CONCLUSION

Healthcare is an evolving field that primarily focuses on ensuring that patients receive quality care to improve their quality of life. Technology has supported the medical staff's ability to enhance the care provided to clients by decreasing physical boundaries to access and intervening early in disease and illness detection. Patients have the power to control their medical needs and access healthcare staff with increased convenience and power to remain in control of how their medical data is accessed and used. Healthcare workers work tirelessly to treat patients, which may lead to burnout.

Technology has built a bridge that will limit repetitive tasks that need to be completed and streamline documentation processes. Healthcare and its connectedness to technology have limitless possibilities for patients to increase healthcare access and outcomes for individuals and communities.

CHAPTER SUMMARIES

- AI has been instrumental in developing NLP within healthcare. NLP is a category within AI that uses algorithms and models capable of assessing language.
- Cloud computing involves collecting data using remote services and managing and storing patient healthcare records and information.
- Predictive technology uses machine learning techniques by monitoring a system and relaying it to a human response.
- Genomic medicine can assist with technology that identifies facial features to aid in the early detection of genetic disorders.
- CRISPR research is an emerging practice area within the biological and medical fields.
- Educational leaders must consider how changes in nanotechnology will impact students' roles in the workplace.
- Technology that can be connected to individuals can assist with monitoring a person's health needs.
- Smart eyewear collects data about clients using sensors embedded in the frames of the glasses.
- Using digital technology to communicate and perform consultations, medical examinations, or interdisciplinary collaboration falls under the medical service of telemedicine.

- Delivering therapy through telerehabilitation is growing, especially for those that live in rural areas. Smartphones and tablets have led to the emergence of the Rehabilitation IoT in a person's home.
- VR and AR have impacted how technology is used in healthcare settings and teaching applications.
- Predictive technology also creates opportunities for the early detection of disease or illness by quickly reviewing client data to note changes in medical stats that can alter medical professionals to a potential problem before symptoms may occur.
- A blockchain is a system used to generate and store data securely.
- AI and healthcare complement one another as medical professionals see the direct benefit of reduced workload, which heightens productivity.
- The amount of time spent in the classroom will decrease, as virtual learning will allow students to be in control of identify the best environment to learn in their natural setting.

REFERENCES

Ayre, K., Bittar, A., Kam, J., Verma, S., Howard, L. M., & Dutta, R. (2021). Developing a natural language processing tool to identify perinatal self-harm in electronic healthcare records. *PLOS ONE, 16*(8), e0253809. https://doi.org/10.1371/journal.pone.0253809

Baclic, O., Tunis, M., Young, K., Doan, C., & Swerdfeger, H. (2020). Challenges and opportunities for public health made possible by advances in natural language processing. *Canada Communicable Disease Report, 46*(6), 161–168. https://doi.org/10.14745/ccdr.v46i06a02

Battineni, G., Sagaro, G., Chinatalapudi, N., & Amenta, F. (2020). Applications of machine learning predictive models in the chronic disease diagnosis. *Journal of Personalized Medicine, 10*(2), 21. https://doi.org/10.3390/jpm10020021

Benjamin. R. M. (2011). An important time for prevention. *Public Health Reports, 126*(1), 2–3. https://doi.org/10.1177/003335491112600102

Bohr, A., & Memarzadeh, K. (2020). The rise of artificial intelligence in healthcare applications. *Artificial Intelligence in Healthcare,* 25–60. https://doi.org/10.1016/b978-0-12-818438-7.00002-2

Botelle, R., Bhavsar, V., Kadra-Scalzo, G., Mascio, A., Williams, M. V., Roberts, A., Velupillai, S., & Stewart, R. (2022). Can natural language processing models extract and classify instances of interpersonal violence in mental healthcare electronic records: An applied evaluative study. *BMJ Open, 12*(2), 911–921. https://doi.org/10.1136/

Datta, S., Sherva, R., De La Cruz, M., Long, M., Roy, P., Backman, V., Chowdhury, S., & Roy, H. (2018). Single nucleotide polymorphism facilitated down-regulation of the cohesion stromal antigen-1: Implications for colorectal cancer racial disparities. *Neoplasia, 20*(3), 289–294. https://doi.org/10.1016/j.neo.2018.01.003

Dias, R., & Torkamani, A. (2019). Artificial intelligence in clinical and genomic diagnostics. *Genome Medicine, 11*(1). https://doi.org/10.1186/s13073-019-0689-8

Dobkin, B. (2017). A rehabilitation-Internet of things in the home to augment motor skills and exercise training. *Neurorehabilitation and Neural Repair, 31*(3), 217–227. https://journals.sagepub.com/doi/10.1177/1545968316680490bmjopen-2021–052911

Garson, A., & Levin, S. (2001). Ten 10-year trends for the future of healthcare: Implications for academic health centers. *The Ochsner Journal, 3*, 10–15. https://www.ncbi.nlm.nih.gov/pmc/articles/PMC3116776/pdf/i1524-5012-3-1-10.pdf

Goodyear, V., Armour, K., & Wood, H. (2018). Young people learning about health: The role of apps and wearable devices. *Learning, Media and Technology, 44*(2), 193–210. https://doi.org/10.1080/17439884.2019.1539011

Guo, P., Yang, J., Huang, J., Auguste, D., & Moses, M. (2019). Therapeutic genome editing of triple negative breast tumors using a non cationic and deformable nanolipogel. *Proceeding of the National Academy of Sciences, 116*(37), 18295–18303. 10.1073/pnas.1904697116

Guo, Y., Hao, Z., Zhao, S., Gong, J., & Yang, F. (2020). Artificial intelligence in health care: Bibliometric analysis. *Journal of Medical Internet Research, 22*(7), 182–228. https://doi.org/10.2196/18228

Haick, H., & Tang, N. (2021). Artificial intelligence in medical sensors for clinical decisions. *ACS Nano, 15*(3), 3557–3567. https://doi.org/10.1021/acsnano.1c00085

Hunnicutt, M., Johnston, R., & Stauble, J. (2018). Genome development: Medical. In S. Staat (Ed.), *Facing and exponential future: Technology and the community college* (pp. 65-76). Rowman & Littlefield.

Kumar, A., Pujari, P., & Gupta, N. (2021). Artificial intelligence: Technology 4.0 as a solution for healthcare workers during COVID-19 pandemic. *Acta Universitatis Bohemiae Meridionalis, 24*(1), 19–35. https://doi.org/10.32725/acta.2021.002

Li, Z., Zheng, Q., Wang, Z., & Li, Z. (2020). Nanogenerator-based self-powered sensors for wearable and implantable electronics. *Research, 2020*, 1–25. https://doi.org/10.34133/2020/8710686

Lui, L. (2018). Occupational therapy in the fourth industrial revolution. *Canadian Journal of Occupational Therapy, 85*(4), 272–285. https://doi.org/10.1177/0008417418815179

National Human Gonome Research Institute (NHGRI). (2019). *NHGRI history and timeline of events*. Genome.gov. Retrieved July 2, 2022, from https://www.genome.gov/about-nhgri/Brief-History-Timeline

Noorbakhsh-Sabet, N., Zand, R., Zhang, Y., & Abedi, V. (2019). Artificial intelligence transforms the future of health care. *The American Journal of Medicine, 132*(7), 795–801. https://doi.org/10.1016/j.amjmed.2019.01.017

Mamdiwar, S., R, A., Shakruwala, Z., Chadha, U., Srinivasan, K., & Chang, C. (2021). Recent advances on IoT-assisted wearable sensor systems for healthcare monitoring. *Biosensors, 11*(10), 372–409. https://doi.org/10.3390/bios11100372

Pacis, D. M. M., Subido, E. D. C., & Bugtai, N. T. (2018). Trends in telemedicine utilizing artificial intelligence. AIP Conference Proceedings. Maharashtra, India. https://doi.org/10.1063/1.5023979

Patel, M., & Gonsalves, F. (2022). Virtual reality and augmented reality in medical science. *International Research Journal of Modernization in Engineering Technology and Science, 4*, 6.

Pottle, J. (2019). Virtual reality and the transformation of medical education. *Future Healthcare Journal, 6*(3), 181–185. https://doi.org/10.7861/fhj.2019-0036

Powell, J. (2019). Trust me, I'm a chatbot: How artificial intelligence in health care fails the turing test. *Journal of Medical Internet Research, 21*(10). https://doi.org/10.2196/16222

Quazi, S. (2022). Artificial intelligence and machine learning in precision and genomic medicine. *Medical Oncology, 39*(8). https://doi.org/10.1007/s12032-022-01711-1

Rawat, B., Bist, A. S., Supriyanti, D., Elmanda, V., & Sari, S. N. (2022). AI and nanotechnology for healthcare: A survey. *APTISI Transactions on Management (ATM), 7*(1), 86–91. https://doi.org/10.33050/atm.v7i1.1819

Sabry, F., Eltaras, T., Labda, W., Alzoubi, K., & Malluhi, Q. (2022). Machine learning for healthcare wearable devices: The big picture. *Journal of Healthcare Engineering, 2022*, 1–25. https://doi.org/10.1155/2022/4653923

Siyal, A. A., Junejo, A. Z., Zawish, M., Ahmed, K., Khalil, A., & Soursou, G. (2019). Applications of blockchain technology in medicine and healthcare: Challenges and future perspectives. *Cryptography, 3*(1), 3. https://doi.org/10.3390/cryptography3010003

Thimbleby, H. (2013). Technology and the future of healthcare. *Journal of Public Health Research, 2*(3), 2013–2028. https://doi.org/10.4081/jphr.2013.e28

Vatandsoost, M., & Litkouhi, S. (2019). The future of healthcare facilities: How technology and medical advances may shape hospitals of the future. *Hospital Practices and Research, 4*(1), 1–11. https://doi.org/10.15171/hpr.2019.01

Wiens, J., & Shenoy, E. (2017). Machine learning for healthcare: On the verge of a major shift in healthcare epidemiology. *Clinical Infectious Diseases, 66*(1), 149–153. https://doi.org/10.1093/cid/cix731

Chapter 7

Artificial Intelligence and Religion

Angela Davis-Baxter

Christians who are in touch with their faith and their current societal events understand that the message has not changed, but the delivery method has. The day of the house-to-house evangelist, often referred to as the Circuit Rider, ended many years ago; therefore, the day of house-to-house evangelism has nearly come to a glorious end. Both digital and electronic platforms must be engaged to serve this present age. The ultimate proof of the necessity of diverse offerings of religious information was demonstrated during the Covid-19 lockdowns. For many, the gospel would have become inaccessible if it had not been for social media platforms.

Technology entered during the creation of the world in the Old Testament book of Genesis. God gave Adam and Eve the ability to build and nurture, distinguishing them from the rest of creation. Thus, early technology was used in the form of tools used to cultivate the land.

> While technology influences and changes us over time, technology is a tool that God has given us to be used in ways that honor him and help us love our neighbor (Matthew 22:37–39). It is true that certain pieces of technology are created for evil and can have an outsized influence on our lives. (Hayner & Thacker, 2019)

God intended for technology to be in the world and allowed man to create tools that enable everyone to live out the greatest commandments (Matt. 22:34–40, New Revised Standard Version,). Technology is a gift from him, brought about by his skilled image-bearers, and should be used to know him better, build up our neighbors, and glorify him above all (Hayner & Thacker, 2019). So, Noah builds a boat large enough to house pairs of all the animals then in the world. It is assumed that he built it with wood, but even so it was quite a project that really demonstrated that construction technology was evident in the early times.

HISTORY OF RELIGION AND TECHNOLOGY

"Technology is as old as humanity, and it is not technics which has created the modern man, but it is the modern man who has created technics" (Brunner, 1949, p. 2). For example, humankind was given the ability to use his or her intelligence to rise beyond nature. The age of technology influencing religious entities is seen with the invention of the printing press, which allowed churches to communicate with their membership. However, during the first industrial revolution, a person's faith and beliefs were shifted to a more robust way of living, leading to a decline in religious leaders' ability to influence people to attend church and other gatherings.

According to White (1995), ". . . religion and technology should not be perceived as opposed to each other, but mutually beneficial. The development of technology significantly impacted liturgical text and calendar, biotechnology of disease control, revised funeral rises, and the rise of congregational studies" (p. 605). The age of technology began with the invention of the printing press, which allowed churches to communicate with their membership. However, during the first industrial revolution, a person's faith shifted to a more robust way of living, leading to a decline in religious leaders' ability to influence people.

The Shift in Theological Education

"The COVID-19 pandemic did not stop at national borders. It has affected people regardless of nationality, level of education, income, or gender. Nevertheless, the same has not been true for its consequences, which have hit the most vulnerable hardest" (Schleicher, 2020, p. 4). March 2020 will forever leave a lasting impact on the higher education system. The news that educational institutions across the United States were closing in-person learning due to Covid-19 left many institutions in an indeterminate state of operation.

Impact on Seminaries

There were several issues seminaries had to consider when transitioning to a remote learning environment including the background and demographic areas of students, faculty, and staff. The seminary acknowledged these individuals came from various backgrounds, but overall, all persons were in the same situation regarding learning and Covid-19. The seminary community worked hard to accommodate students, faculty, and staff with virtual learning by supporting their anxieties and concerns.

"This crisis has exposed the many inadequacies and inequities in the education system from access to the broadband and computers needed for online education to the supportive environments needed to focus on learning, and the misalignment between resources and needs." (Schleicher, 2020 p. 4). However, serving students during a pandemic required schools to consider and apply an innovative learning approach. Thus, evaluating the student population makeup is crucial in finding the best method for instruction and meeting student services' needs.

The pandemic widely impacted seminary's traditional teaching style and field experiences. It reminded the institution that students were affected differently regarding their ability to transition to remote learning. First, the population of students whom the seminary serves include pastors overseeing congregations, ministers in specialized areas, chaplains, other clergy, and lay leaders. The population of students comes primarily from churches with a median age of fifty across North and South Carolina.

Many student pastors in rural churches had little to no technology prior to the onset of the pandemic. Students were faced with navigating their churches from in-person worship to remote worship via conference call, Zoom, and Facebook while scrambling to transition to a new learning format at the seminary. Moreover, students differ from one another with diverse backgrounds, resources, and support outside of the institution.

Although the pandemic changed the institution's learning environment, some students could adapt to the crisis because they had the proper resources and were more familiar with online learning. While ministry is about people and has traditionally been demonstrated in face-to-face and via in-person connections, the seminary was forced to tailoring its teaching format to remain relevant, while reinventing the learning process to expand student-teacher relationships to serve the present age with the disruption of Covid-19.

Institutions had to develop strategies to promote the learning and development of faculty and students. A significant feature of any college is the ability to supply technology. However, the institution must analyze technology's importance and benefit without the fear of being left behind. Colleges will continue to meet the demands and adjust to the changes within the technology arena.

Online education is being done in three ways. First, by learning and adopting digital software and platforms by teachers and students; second, by preparing academic notes, video, and audio educational materials; third, by using the digital platform for assessment and evaluation. Traditional classroom and teaching system has changed with redefining roles during online classes. (Mohapatra, 2020, p. 5)

Although the pandemic has obstructed students from all academic disciplines, seminary students have felt unique pressure as they discern calls to enter positions and places of worship that may not resemble what they did before the virus appeared. Clergy students are often faced with deciding whether to attend class or nurture their congregations through this global crisis. The pandemic has added an additional layer of considerations for seminary students to discern how to manage and balance school, church, and other ministerial responsibilities. Seminaries must provide the necessary technical resources to accommodate the realities student encounters.

TECHNOLOGY AND RELIGIOUS PROGRAMS IN 2032

Institutions over the past several years realized the need for more online and hybrid learning courses to allow opportunities for students across the globe to obtain a theological education. As a result, enrollment in theological colleges has increased because of the implementation of new ways of learning. Students play a vital role in deciding what courses are needed to meet their congregation's and community's needs. For seminaries and religious studies programs to survive in theological education, a new foundation must continue to build new innovative programs and services to promote a learning culture (O'Banion, 1997).

Over the past 20-plus years, the development of technology has affected how ministerial leaders, theological educators, and institutions trained individuals for pastoral appointments, clinical positions, chaplaincy, counseling, and social justice advocacy. A traditional seminary education was based on face-to-face classroom time and practical field internships; however, the advancement of technology changed the original structure to virtual opportunities. For example, colleges and churches use multiple screens, websites, live-streaming, video announcements, sound effects, and more to train and minister to individuals.

Technology Streams

Today, religious colleges use many forms of technology in collaboration with their teaching format. For example, in learning management systems, students can hold group meetings and discuss course assignments and projects on one another's work using discussion boards, blogs, chatrooms, Zoom sessions and the like. In addition, those learning tools enable students to engage with faculty and other students within the class at any given day or time. In 2032, technology will impact the field of theological education to align with how religious institutions provide instruction.

The learning format will continue through Zoom, videos, discussion boards, chat rooms, learning management systems, and independent learning. However, faculty members will shift to engage various forms of artificial intelligence (AI) to teach the biblical languages, Greek, Hebrew, and New and Old Testament courses. Students will learn the languages at their own pace through virtual design learning formats. Theological educational institutions will require intense research on AI and the learning process for educating ministers, to effectively serve humanity and meet the challenges of an ever-evolving world.

The impact of AI and its effect on human identity will change humans' roles, aspirations, and fulfillment. AI will create changes that will affect the knowledgeable and unknowledgeable regarding technology. Knowledgeable persons will build it, train it, and regulate the use of AI through the breakthroughs of technologies. However, those who are unknowledgeable about AI will be gratified by its capabilities to communicate with their parishioners, attend virtual courses, share worship experiences, and connect with other believers throughout the globe.

Communication Tools

Communication tools are essential for distance and online students to attend lectures, meet the instructor, get to know other students in class, interact with the instructors and peers, perform learning tasks, and form online learning communities that connect learners at various locations. In addition, communication technology tools allow instructors to deliver lectures efficiently, facilitate discussions, and offer office hours to on and off-campus students.

The Metaverse

In 2032, the Metaverse will commence entering the area of theological education. "Metaverse appears for the first time in the novel *Snow Crash*, published in 1992 by cyberpunk writer Neal Stephenson. Metaverses are virtual spaces for real world recreation where users, normally under an avatar or a pseudonym, interact with other users in endless everyday situations" (Diaz et al., 2020, p. 94). Metaverse is a three-dimensional virtual AI technology that allows people to interact with each other socially and economically, regardless of their location, using computational tools.

Diaz et al. (2020) says, ". . . identifies three attributes of the metaverse artificial intelligence technology. First, interactivity allows the user to interact with the metaverse. The behavior of operators can impact on the objects and the on the behaviors of others" (p. 95). This interaction will take place on Snapchat, Instagram, and Facebook to explore personal and global connections (Diaz et al., 2020). Second, "avatars represent corporeity users. Corporeity consists in the presence of that avatar in that space that also has limits since it is subject to certain laws and has limited resources within the virtual world" (Diaz et al., 2020, p. 95).

Avatar restrictions are often due to a shortage of computing resources in the virtual world. Third, the "persistence program continues to function and develop even though its members are not connected. In addition, the position, conversations, and property objects are saved and will be retrieved once the user is reconnected to the virtual world" (Diaz et al., 2020, p. 96). On the other hand, Hwang & Chien (2021), describes "the importance of artificial intelligence and the metaverse to ensure that the world of metaverse functions follow the rules defined by the creator" (p. 2). Three artificial bits of intelligence are needed for the Metaverse.

> For example, in a metaverse-based game, there are likely to be competitions or fights; thus, arbitration is needed to judge who wins and who loses and determine the consequences. Simulation is when a user grows plants or raises animals; there is the need for a simulation function to determine the status of the plants or animals as time passes. The AI module also needs to make decisions following the rules pre-defined by the creator, such as determining the consequences when some events happen based on the pre-defined rules. (Hwang & Chien, 2021, p. 2)

Metaverse and Education

The Metaverse can influence higher educational medical, nursing, healthcare education, science, military training, manufacturing, and language learning (Hwang & Chien, 2022, p. 2). In addition, this revolution will afford theological educational institutions different ways to educate students. In 2032, the Metaverse will be an exploratory technology among religious colleges and seminaries but not the sole purpose for learning. "Moreover, the metaverse in education is an authentic world that enables learners to work and learn with intelligent NPC tutors, peers, and tutees as well as other human learners" (Hwang & Chien, 2021, p. 2).

Non-Players

The non-player characteristics (NPC) in the Metaverse act like humans, which is needed for decision-making. First, the NPC tutor provides users a method asking for help from those individuals who are knowledgeable or experienced. Unfortunately, there may be circumstances where the pupil cannot locate a user to resolve a problem. Second, the NPC tutee/student serves as a resource for practicing teaching others and training as a mentor. "For example, for a learner who is a pre-service teacher, he or she might need to practice his or her class management or learning design skills" (Hwang & Chien, 2021, p. 3).

Third, the NPC peer is important where leaders interact with their peers. "An ideal case is that several users are experiencing and learning in the same contexts for the same educational purposes so that they can discuss with each other during the learning process" (Hwang & Chien, 2021, p. 3). Technology advancement in the Metaverse in 2032 will shift technological education into a new teaching and learning arena. Adapting to this new technology will require creative teaching styles, financial resources, and commitments from seminary presidents and religious institution leaders to change their habitual thinking to an innovative approach to learning.

THE YEAR 2050 AND ARTIFICIAL INTELLIGENCE

Scripture in Ecclesiastes 1:9 states: "There is nothing new under the Sun" (New Revised Standard Version). Therefore, in the year 2050, believers' character and faith will be developed and tested. America will undergo more pandemics, tragedies, and technological advancements. The Covid-19 virus of 2020 shattered the lives of more than one million people worldwide, gun violence has increased at an all-time high; the overturning of Roe v. Wade, the debate of gun laws, and justice disparities challenged the function of the universal church, believers, and clergy.

During that time, the modern church learned and acted on how to be the church without being physically present in the structured building. Because of the Covid-19 pandemic and the social unrest in America and globally, the Universal Church realized that a virtual meeting using a method like Zoom could become a kind of church sanctuary. Moreover, in the author's opinion, the world is watching, and the universal church will be judged as to whether it found innovative ways to meet its congregants' natural and spiritual needs.

AI and Education in 2050

By 2050, AI is the way of life for humans and the advancement of technologies for the present and future. Thus, the progression of AI is developed with visual recognition, algorithms, and codes that go beyond the human scope (Kissinger et al., 2021). For example, Metaverse technology will dominate theological education to help students emerge themselves into action-oriented technology. Subsequently, the reinforcement learning through AI will be determined by the environment, observation, and recording responses to actions.

"The metaverse enables learners to have more opportunities to experience, explore, learn, and teach in a new world, as well as working and interacting with people" (Hwang & Chien, 2021, p. 3). Thus, the Metaverse platform will offer adventures for individuals who cannot experience them in real life. According to Hwang & Chien (2021), educational institutions will benefit from the Metaverse.

1. To constantly situate learners in a cognitive or skill-practicing environment . . .
2. To enable learners to . . . learn something that requires long-term involvement . . .
3. To encourage learners to create something they cannot afford in the real world . . .
4. To enable learners to have alternative thoughts and attempts regarding their careers . . .
5. To enable learners to experience . . . things from different perspectives or roles.
6. To enable learners to learn to collaborate with people . . .
7. To explore learners' potential or higher-order thinking . . . (p. 3).

As Metaverse development expands, seminaries and colleges will equip this technology with necessary AI data to produce relevant theological teachings for students. The framework for theological education and the Metaverse will depend on the need of the universal church. The diversity of students requires incorporating curricula geared toward embracing all cultures to equip men and women as active ministers within their communities. Additionally, using the Metaverse will give students pastoral care and counseling field experiences without leaving their homes.

Learners' Performance and Metaverse

Theological institutions will evaluate the Metaverse method via data from interactive sessions within the Metaverse platform. A database will automatically send information to professors with detailed information regarding a student's Metaverse participatory time, lessons accomplished, and peer interaction between students. Also, students will use the Metaverse to meet as a class with the professor providing an interactive exchange between the faculty member and the class. Each institution will establish guidelines for teaching using the Metaverse platform:

by adopting the metaverse-based educational approach, learners can have continuous learning opportunities without being limited by space and time, as well as receiving full support or guidance for making reflections based on the analysis results of their learning logs. When adopting a new technology for educational purposes, many personal factors, such as learners' knowledge levels, cognitive styles, preferences, learning motivations, self-efficacy, and learning attitudes, could affect their acceptance or performance in the new technological contexts. (Hwang & Chien, 2021, p. 4)

Theological Education Theories and Metaverse

As Metaverse becomes dominant in 2050, it is essential to remember the framework for establishing a Metaverse platform. First, the roles of AI in the Metaverse will need to be considered when integrating the Metaverse into a curriculum program. "For example, based on the feature 'shared,' social constructivism, which emphasizes that one's knowledge is constructed through social interactions, could be a good choice for supporting the use of the metaverse in educational settings" (Hwang & Chien, 2021, p. 3).

Institutions must understand that combining Metaverse into a learning format will require strategic planning among faculty, technology specialists, and leaders. Because the role of the clergyperson is empathy, the Metaverse will give learners authentic situations that allow them to experience the entire ministerial process, including burial, baptism, marriage, sermons, Bible study, and decision-making. They will experience the reality of the full gamut of pastoral service as well as consequences of their decisions. The area of Christian education will promote activities for adults and children through the metaverse learning technology.

Students will learn how to engage children and teenagers in activities at virtual church while educating them on biblical principles. Vacation Bible School and Bible study will look different because students graduating from seminary education will use Metaverse as a standard for teaching rather than paper, email, Zoom, lectures, and video chats. Moreover, pastors and religious leaders will be able to better serve individuals with disabilities through innovative hand-and-eye correction activities and specialized areas for learning. The Metaverse development will not be easy for theological institutions.

Leaders must create a Metaverse framework and implement autonomous robots to remain functional. Overall, "due to the richness and powerful technology of the metaverse, it should be seen not just as a game or experience, but as a highly complex community" (Hwang & Chien, 2021, p. 4).

Robots and the Future of Religion 2050

Historically, some colleges were founded by church denominations; so, the birth of religious education often began in liberal arts colleges. The church was once a place where family and friends worshipped and fellowshipped; however, by 2050, the church had become a place of worship that may occur anywhere and at any time. Seminaries and religious colleges experienced a decline in human demand for a pastor due to the number of persons opting out of attending in-person church. The human-like robot took the place of pastors, chaplains, and other religious leaders in the pulpit, hospital, hospice, pastoral care and counseling, and social justice.

The autonomous robots influence how individuals receive their education at a religious institution. For example, a professor teaching an Old Testament course will work with a robot to teach the course. In addition, robots have become the dominant method for teaching students inside the classroom. Therefore, program development will center around the inclusion of robots teaching all levels of theology.

The Function of Robots and Religion

"Robots are expected to fulfill a role of support in human life; the appearance of robots is a matter of critical importance to facilitate interaction with people" (Trovato, et al., 2021, p. 540). Furthermore, because seminaries teach compassion and empathy, robots teaching at the institution are designed to teach students the necessary skills for serving as ministerial leaders. More importantly, robots are capable of determining the culture of students and what is needed to meet the needs of each student.

> Robots and religion as the synthesis of the two extremes can be better understood by looking at the field of Angelology. For centuries, theologians and philosophers across various religions spent effort studying angels. Angels are without a soul; therefore, humanoid robotics could be considered specular, as it is the study of "body without a soul," and it leads to a deeper understanding of human nature, especially thanks to the realization of androids. (Trovato et al., 2021, p. 540–541)

Robots are designed to cultivate the understanding of humans in the field of education. "The Theomorphic Robot is related to the fact that religion is intertwined with culture, and divine representations that are present in world culture and are familiar especially to believers, but also not non-believers" (Trovato et al., 2021, p. 549). Because individuals have experienced a calling from God or a higher being, it will be essential for theological institutions to create robots with similar characteristics. The Design Guidelines for

Theomorphic Robots will pay attention to religion and religious practices, the sacredness of the robot, abstract reviews, and the spirituality of one's belief (Trovato et al., 2021).

The robotic age is here in 2050, and religious institutions and organizations use various robots to interact with humans. Robots are determining what is needed to aid people in their faith and belief effectively. Robots are in people's lives and perform religious duties that a pastor often holds. ". . . the widespread acceptance of robots can give rise to a market for religious robots that cater to the specific needs of different religious devotees, e.g., Christianity, Judaism, Islam, Hinduism, Buddhism, etc." (Ahmend & Manh, 2021, p. 228).

Ahmend & Manh (2021) describe how robots serve institutions and organizations. Robots serve as teaching instruments with knowledge of religion, ethics, pastoral care, and counseling courses. The AI of robots can make cognitive and intellectual decisions when facilitating classroom instruction. Since a significant responsibility of ministerial leaders is to provide counseling, properly designed robots will provide counseling to individuals around death, marriage, birth, gender differences, and the scriptures.

"Religious assistant robots physically assist the religious figureheads in the accomplishment of everyday life chores and activities in the church, synagogues, mosques, and temples" (Ahmend & Manh, 2021, p. 228). Theological schools will teach more companionship courses due to the advancement of medicine, and people living longer will require institutions to create religious companion robots. Because humans engage in social functions, incorporating social robots into the educational framework will give students a sense of belonging in the theological environment.

CONCLUSION

Humans will always be the foundation for religion and its connection with the world. However, humans in the 2050s encounter the use of robots within the religious community, and theomorphic robots will impact the way organizations teach and experience religion. Although religious robots will be in most religious organizations, concerns of ethical and social discrimination implications may impede one's faith. While using the Metaverse for educational purposes provides an effective learning mode, it could also raise ethical issues. Nonetheless, Christian seminaries and theological institutions will continue to carry out its mission.

CHAPTER SUMMARIES

- Both digital and electronic platforms must be engaged to serve this present age.
- God intended for technology to be in the world and allowed man to create tools that enable everyone to live out the greatest commandments.
- Although the pandemic changed the institution's learning environment, some students could adapt to the crisis because they had the proper resources and were more familiar with online learning.
- A traditional seminary education was based on face-to-face classroom time and practical field internships; however, the advancement of technology changed the original structure to virtual opportunities.
- The learning format will continue through Zoom, videos, discussion boards, chat rooms, learning management systems, and independent learning.
- In 2032, the Metaverse will commence entering the area of theological education.
- AI is the way of life for humans and the advancement of technologies for the present and future.
- Theological institutions will evaluate the Metaverse method via data from interactive sessions within the Metaverse platform.
- Institutions must understand that combining metaverse into a learning format will require strategic planning among faculty, technology specialist, and leaders.
- The autonomous robots influence how individuals receive their education at a religious institution.
- The Design Guidelines for Theomorphic Robots will pay attention to religion and religious practices, the sacredness of the robot, abstract reviews, and the spirituality of one's belief.

REFERENCES

Ahmed, H., & Manh, L. (2021). Evaluating the co-dependence and co-existence between religion and robots: past, present, and insights on the future. *International Journal of Social Robotics, 13(2),* 219–235. DOI:10.1007/s12369-020-00636-x.

Brunner, E. (1949). *Christianity and civilization.* Charles Scribner's Sons.

Diaz, M., Eduardo, J., Andres, C., Saldana, D., Avila, R., & Alberto, C. (2020). Virtual world as a resource for hybrid education. *International Journal of Emerging Technologies in Learning (Online); Vienna, 15*(15), 94–109. DOI:10.3991/ijet. v15i15.13025

Hayner, C., & Thacker, J. (2019). *What does the Bible teaches us about technology?* The Ethics & Religious Liberty Commission of the Southern Baptist Convention. https://erlc.com/resource-library/articles/what-does-the-bible-teach-us-about-technology/

Kissinger, H.A., Schmidt, E., & Huttenlocher, D. (2021). The age of AI and our human future. Little Brown and Company.

Mohapatra, A.K. (2020). Editorial: Impact of Covid-19 on higher education. *Journal of Management & Public Policy, 11*(2), 4–6.

New Revised Standard Version of the Bible. (1989). Harper-Collins, Publisher.

O'Banion, T. (1997). *A learning college for the 21st century.* American Council on Education and the Onyx Press.

Schleicher, A. (2020). The impact of Covid-19 on education. Insights from education at a glance 2020, 1–31. https://www.oecd.org/education/the-impact-of-covid-19-on-education-insights-education-at-a-glance-2020.pdf

Trovato, G., Chamas, L., Nishimura, M., Paredes, R., Lucho, C., Huerta-Mercado, A., & Cuellar, F. (2021). Religion and robots: Towards the synthesis of two extremes. *International Journal of Social Robotics, 13,* 539–556. https://doi.org/10.1007/s12369-019-00553-8

White, S. (1995), Christian worship and technological change. *Theological Studies, 56*(3), 605.

Epilogue

By the time this book is published, AI will have moved toward it goals in 2032. There is literally nothing to stop it. In the United States, most likely inventors, innovators, and entrepreneurs will search for and find new ways to use the powerful computer potential. Quantum computing when combined with AI will move it ahead at more than a breathtaking velocity. On the other hand, if for some unforeseen reasons Americans decided to ignore it, scientists and engineers will continue to develop AI in China, Russia, South Korea, Japan, and the European countries.

There is no way to halt the development of AI and any of the other 21-century technologies; they will continue to grow like weeds in field of corn. It is critical that the educators at all levels, and higher education in particular, become aware of what the possibilities are by researching all that is known about AI and then plan ways to use it for helping to educate human beings on our planet in the middle of space. AI will help us explore the moon, take excursions to Mars, and travel to all places known and unknown in the universe and beyond. It is only a matter of time.

About the Editor and Contributors

Darrel W. Staat received his doctorate from the University of Michigan, master's degree from Western Michigan University, and bachelor's degree from Hope College. He has taught a series of eight undergraduate courses and six graduate courses. After retirement, and finding it not to his liking, he assumed the position of coordinator and faculty member in Wingate University's Higher Education Executive Leadership program in January 2015.

Currently he holds the position of coordinator and associate professor of the Higher Education Executive Leadership program. Previously, he held the positions of president of the South Carolina Technical College System in Columbia, South Carolina; president of Central Virginia Community College in Lynchburg, Virginia; the founding president of York County Community College in Wells, Maine; and president of Eastern Maine Community College in Bangor, Maine.

His previous publications include:

Centers of Excellence: Niche Methods to Improve Higher Education (2022)
Leading the Community College: Pathways Through an Exponentially Digital Age (2022)
Virtual Reality in Higher Education: Instruction in an Exponential Digital Age (2021)
Higher Education Planning in an Exponential Age: A Continuous, Dynamic Process (2021)
Student Focused Learning: Higher Education in an Exponential Digital Era (2020)
A Baseline of Development: Higher Education and Technology (2019)
Exponential Technologies: Higher Education in an Era of Serial Disruptions (2019)
Facing an Exponential Future: Technology and the Community College (2018)

* * *

Angela Davis-Baxter holds a master's degrees in Divergent Learning, and Educational Leadership, and an Ed.S. in higher administration. She is currently the associate director of Human Services at Hood Theological Seminary in Salisbury, North Carolina.

Kateryna Decker holds two master's degrees, one in Instructional Design and Technology and a second in Foundations of Education and Ed.S. in higher administration. She is currently the Instructional Technology and Design Consultant at Wingate University in Wingate, North Carolina.

Paul Mills holds a master's degree in English Literature and an Ed.S. in higher administration. He is currently a faculty member at Brunswick Community College in Supply, North Carolina.

Jeff Parsons holds two master's degrees, one in Mechanical Engineering, and a second in Christian Studies, and an Ed.S. in higher administration. He is currently the vice president of Academic Affairs at Stanly Community College in Albemarle, North Carolina.

Jannyelle Pitter holds a master's degree in Occupation Therapy and an Ed.S. in higher administration. She is currently the Academic Field Coordinator for Occupational Therapy at Pfeiffer University in Albemarle, North Carolina.

Demetria Smith holds a master's degree in Higher Education Administration and an Ed.S. in higher administration. She is currently the associate director for Student Engagement: Fraternity and Sorority at East Carolina University in Greenville, North Carolina.

Shenika Ward holds a master's degree in School Counseling and an Ed.S. in higher administration. She is currently the dean of Diversity and Cultural Planning at Sand Hills Community College in Pinehurst, North Carolina.

Milton Keynes UK
Ingram Content Group UK Ltd.
UKHW041546231123
433135UK00004B/30